D0045242

The Cole Porter Story

Books for Young People
by David Ewen

THE COLE PORTER STORY

WITH A SONG IN HIS HEART
The Story of Richard Rodgers

THE STORY OF ARTURO TOSCANINI

HAYDN: A Good Life

TALES FROM THE VIENNA WOODS
The Story of Johann Strauss

THE STORY OF JEROME KERN

THE STORY OF IRVING BERLIN

THE STORY OF GEORGE GERSHWIN

The Cole Porter Story

by David Ewen

Holt, Rinehart and Winston

New York Chicago San Francisco

Published simultaneously in Canada by Holt, Rinehart
and Winston of Canada, Limited.
Library of Congress Catalog Card Number: 65-21542
First Edition
92625-2115
Printed in the United States of America

Contents

Prologue
Yesterday & Today

THE FRENCH HAVE A SAYING that goes: "The more things change, the more they stay the same."

The nineteen-twenties are a case in point. Movies, television, and books have recreated this colorful era vividly as an abandoned period—"frenzied," "turbulent," "roaring" is the way it has been described. It was all of these things. But were the nineteen-twenties so different from our own times?

The teen-agers of that decade were known as the "lost generation" and those of our own decade are called the "beat generation." A rose by any other name . . . members of the young set of the twenties were often referred to as "flappers," or "cake-eaters," or "sheiks"; those of today, as "beatniks." The descriptive words may differ, but the connotation remains the same.

In the twenties they danced the Charleston, the Lindy Hop, and the Black Bottom with wild contortions of body, hips, and legs. Today the shaking is pretty much as it was yesterday, though the ritual is now called the "Twist," the "Frug," or the "Watusi." Young people used to do most of their dancing to the music of phonograph records; they are doing so again, in places called "discothèques."

In the twenties, the favored music (they called it "jazz") was regarded by a good many people as the corruption of existing moral and musical values. Today, rock 'n' roll is being condemned in much the same way. And in an article in *Look*—on December 15, 1964—Samuel Grafton claimed that the "jazz age" has come back. He said, "Americans are dancing again, staying up late in night spots to do so, as they have not for many years. Girls are showing their knees, as they did with their rolled stocking tops and flying short skirts in the twenties. Bars are crowded as speakeasies never were. . . . Once again the wail of the saxophone is heard in the land. Even the banjo is back."

In the twenties, Rudy Vallee was a crooning sensation in night clubs and over the radio. Today, Rudy Vallee is still crooning, though most recently in the musical theater rather than over the radio. And some of today's singing idols—say, Frank Sinatra or Perry Como—may not refer to their art as "crooning" (a term that has become obsolete); but to many its appeal rests nonetheless on the same kind of relaxed, subdued, and restrained style that originally made Rudy Vallee so popular.

In the twenties, Clara Bow was the screen sex symbol. They called her the "It" girl—"It" representing sex appeal. Today we have Brigitte Bardot and Elizabeth Taylor as personifications and glorification of female sex attraction.

The twenties were plagued by the "high cost of living." Today we suffer from "inflation." The twenties were partial to fads and foibles: ouija boards, miniature golf, autosuggestion, flagpole sitting, marathon dancing. We haven't changed very much. Stunts and vogues and gimmicks have also taken root in our own day: the hula hoop, packing telephone booths, hot rods. Morals in the twenties were said to have plunged to the lowest depths; literature and the theater were vigorously condemned as pornographic; the family structure was said to have been reduced to nonexistence. Those who judge our society are saying just about the same things today. Theater, movies, TV shows, and paperback books are targets for outraged denunciations by many a citizen who claims that we are dragging both our art and our entertainment through a cesspool. As for ethics—the pay-offs, bribes, and petty deals of the twenties (for example, the Teapot Dome Scandal that reached into the highest echelon of our Government) can today be matched by rigged TV quizzes, "payola," income-tax frauds, and the Bobby Baker scandal.

There is, however, one major way in which our social climate differs from yesterday's. Our own times are a carry-over, or a repetition, if you prefer, of the twenties —even if sometimes with refinements, extensions, transformations, and excesses—while the atmosphere of the twenties was a complete break with the past. This period represented a social revolution that destroyed long-held concepts and values in America, a revolution that glorified a new set of living standards, that gave birth to a new way of life.

Act One
The Roaring Twenties

THE TWENTIES WERE THE AFTERMATH of the most extensive and far-reaching war the world had yet known. Propaganda had promised that this would be the war to end all wars. But as the League of Nations was being sabotaged by the American Congress, and as bickering and quarrels among European nations for the spoils of war were causing friction among one-time Allies, suspicion began to grow among many Americans that perhaps this World War had carried within it the seeds of another, even greater, holocaust. Such a suspicion brought about a disenchantment with idealism, a cynicism toward all things with high purpose, and an iconoclasm toward old ways and thinking habits.

The release from the tensions, fears, and agonies of a war induced a passion for enjoying life to its fullest measure. "Having a good time" became the be-all and end-all of existence, almost a new religion. People were determined to enjoy each waking moment, live for today and not to give a second thought to tomorrow. "In the morning, in the evening, ain't we got fun?" the people sang in 1921. In 1922 they sang, "I'm runnin' wild, I'm runnin' wild"; in 1924, "I want to be happy"; in 1925, "I'm sittin' on top of the world."

An unprecedented wave of prosperity swept over the country as land values and the stock market soared, wages and profits zoomed, and business expanded. People were determined to live high, wide, and handsome; lavishness was the keynote of the moment. Homes were exchanged for mansions. What had been merely convenient methods of transportation became luxurious convertible cars and handsome yachts. Everything was opulent to the point of flamboyance—from the stage sets and costumes of the *Ziegfeld Follies* to the way men and women lived, ate and drank, and dressed. Theaters and night clubs flourished. Restaurants were overcrowded. Everywhere money was being spent as if it were flowing liquid. One of the most popular personalities in the entertainment world was Texas Guinan, the boisterous proprietress of a night club. "Hello, sucker!"

was the way she used to greet her clients. "Suckers" they were—for the prices in her club were astronomic. Nevertheless, the customers grinned, paid, and came back again and again.

Other facets of American life were similarly free and easy, with sex consciousness heightened and intensified not only on the still-silent screen, but also through the glorification of the female with the first Miss America contest in Atlantic City, New Jersey, in 1921. Social freedom was the order of the day, for young *and* old.

The favored pose was a devil-may-care attitude toward most of the things a former generation had respected. Lawlessness spread like contagion. Gangsters and their leaders built fabulous empires on the foundation stones of bribery, terror, and even murder. Such practices were almost considered as basic to free enterprise. Newspapers fattened their circulation through the lurid exploitation of scandals. Everybody enjoyed reading about them, talking about them; but nobody seemed interested in trying to find a remedy for what was a social malignancy.

The truth of the matter was that everybody was too busy accumulating wealth, too busy looking for new ways of spending money, too concerned with having good times to become overly interested in reforms. People behaved as if they were on a New Year's Eve binge —but the binge lasted a decade.

The essence of the twenties was caught and fixed by many different people in many different places and ways: in literature, by the works of writers like F. Scott Fitzgerald, Ernest Hemingway, and Sinclair Lewis; in music, by the symphonic jazz of George Gershwin and Ferde Grofé; in the theater by plays like *Chicago* and *Gentlemen Prefer Blondes* and musical comedies like *Good News;* in journalism by the tabloid and the gossip columnist, both children of the twenties; in poetry, by Dorothy Parker's cynical light verse.

The mood, the spirit, the temper of the twenties were caught by Cole Porter. In his melodies and lyrics (he was one composer who always wrote both) he "fixed the smartness and cynicism, the freedom in sex attitudes, the lack of inhibitions in speech and behavior, and the outright iconoclasm that had characterized the 1920s." That is what I once said in another book, *The Story of America's Musical Theater*, adding: "He is the arch cynic to whom a crushing love affair was 'just one of those things' and who could be true to his loved one 'only in my fashion.' He is the dilettante who sprinkles through his lyrics cultural, literary and geographical allusions of a well-read, well-educated, and well-traveled man. He is the nonconformist unafraid of the erotic, the exotic, or the esoteric. He is the sensualist who brings to his melodies throbbing excitement, purple moods, irresistible climaxes."

Where song writers before the twenties had been tender or sentimental, Cole Porter preferred being witty or urbane; where others had been romantic, he was passionate or disenchanted; where others had been simple, direct, or ingenuous, he was sophisticated, and at times even blasé. Songs like "Night and Day," "Begin the Beguine," "What Is This Thing Called Love?", "Love for Sale," "I've Got You Under My Skin," "Let's Do It," "Let's Misbehave," and "Just One of Those Things" reflect through words and melody many of the attitudes of the twenties. This holds true in spite of the fact that some of these songs were written in the nineteen-thirties. For though the twenties left Porter, Porter never really left the twenties. He carried along with him into more sober times a good deal of the heady intoxication of a bygone era. Yet, strange to say, there is no feeling of anachronism in songs that belong to the twenties, but are still so much a part of the fifties and sixties. Today as yesterday the songs are both meaningful and magical.

In deed as well as in thought, Cole Porter was a child of the twenties. He lived as he wrote. Like a character fabricated by F. Scott Fitzgerald, Porter hunted excitement, adventure, gaiety, the way idealists seek truth and the practical strive for money. He was a sybarite to whom luxury was a necessity.

Provocative, unpredictable, sometimes even irresponsible—but always with laughter on his lips and the joy of living in his heart—Cole Porter was the living symbol of the decade in which he first achieved his full maturity as a song writer.

COLE PORTER WAS BORN to wealth. The place was the little town of Peru, Indiana (population 1,500), seventy-five miles north of Indianapolis in the corn country. The town was too small for a train stop; South Bend had the nearest railroad station. The sole point of civic pride for Peru was that it was the winter home of the Hagenbach and Wallace Circus.

Cole Porter's grandfather—J. O. Cole—had been a pioneer in California during the days of the 1849 gold rush. He did not find any gold then, but later he did manage to make wise coal and timber investments in West Virginia and to build up by 1890 a fortune estimated at $7,000,000. In semiretirement in Peru he allowed his son-in-law, Samuel Fenwick Porter, to run his vast business enterprises. Sam also took care of a 750-acre fruit ranch where he lived with his wife, Kate Cole Porter, and their only child, Cole Albert Porter, born on June 9, 1892.

Several childhood impressions stayed with Cole Porter all his life. One came from his visits to the winter quarters of the circus where he sat enraptured. An acrobat's tricks then seemed to him the highest form of human achievement. "When I grow up," he told his mother one day with finality, "I'm going to be an acrobat."

Another childhood memory was of a picture on the curtain of Peru's only theater—grandiloquently referred to as an "opera-house," though opera was never performed there. A polychrome depicted the Grand Canal in Venice, a gondola drifting toward the Rialto Bridge in the distance. Something about that picture fired his imagination. Venice, he became convinced, must surely be the most beautiful place in the world. It is possible that Porter dreamt of seeing, perhaps even of living in, Venice. It is also possible that this childhood ambition, inspired by a theater curtain, caused him always to regard Venice as his favorite place. Later in life he never seemed able to get enough of the city of canals, no matter how often he returned, or how long he stayed.

Other childhood experiences involved music. Cole's mother, a competent amateur pianist, began teaching him to play the piano when he was six. Before long he combined these lessons with the study of the violin. He played one instrument or the other practically all the time—so engrossed in making music that the games of his young friends bored him and he avoided both games *and* friends. Cole composed his first piece of music when he was ten; even then he wrote the words as well. He called it "The Song of the Birds" and dedicated it to his mother. One year later he produced a piano composition, "The Bobolink Waltz." His mother arranged to have it published in Chicago, but Porter never saw a copy, never received any royalties.

Cole's mother was delighted with her son's musical gift; his father was tolerant of it. But his grandfather—the tycoon—was undisguisedly hostile to what he deemed "nonsense." Cole, his only grandchild, must, he insisted, carry on the financial empire he had built. Absorption with music could only interfere with the plans he had carefully drawn up for the boy. J. O. Cole, therefore, laid down the law. Cole would be permitted to follow his musical inclinations, but only if they did not in any way interfere with his academic work. He wanted Cole to study law at Yale; law, he felt, would be a valuable instrument in the handling of the complex business affairs of the family. To sweeten the dish for the boy, the grandfather promised Cole a sixth of his entire fortune on the day Cole received his law degree.

Before going to Yale, Cole attended Worcester Academy in Worcester, Massachusetts, an exclusive private school. He was brilliant in languages and the arts, somewhat less so in the sciences. But music remained his first love. He was writing melodies all the time, and verses as well. His smart little poems were the delight of his fellow students, who committed them to memory and went around quoting their favorite lines.

At the Worcester Academy graduation ceremonies in 1909, Porter was the class valedictorian. This brought him from his grandfather the reward of a holiday in France, Italy, Switzerland, and Germany. But for Cole, Europe meant first and foremost—Venice. He came, he saw, and he fell in love with it—just as he had fallen in love with its picture years before on the theater curtain in Peru. He also fell in love with Paris at first sight. This love affair with Paris and Venice, begun in 1909, continued for nearly half a century.

In the fall of 1909, Porter entered his freshman year at Yale. Among his classmates were a number of people who would become famous in various fields of endeavor: William Christian Bullitt, later American Ambassador to France; Gerald Murphy, destined to become president of Mark Cross, New York's Fifth Avenue establishment selling leather goods and gift items; T. Lawrason Riggs, a socialite who was to assume the office of Roman Catholic chaplain at Yale University; Monty Woolley, one day to become equally famous for his beard and his gifts as an actor, but who long before that returned to Yale as an English instructor and as a coach for graduate dramatics.

Among these and others from well-to-do families, Cole moved with grace and ease. He became a member of the fashionable Delta Kappa Epsilon fraternity, and of the exclusive Elite of Yale. The "Elite" was a formal club that numbered among its members W. Averell Harriman, later a Governor of New York, and Archibald MacLeish, now a celebrated dramatist and poet.

Porter's fellow students remember him as a slight, sensitive fellow, who lived in a room overcrowded with valises and trunks which he never seemed to open, and a piano which he was always playing. A single shadeless electric bulb provided the only illumination. Gerald Murphy now recalls that Porter was always meticulously groomed; that his nails were ever neatly trimmed and polished; that his manners were always impeccable; and that he exuded charm effortlessly. Even in those college years he was a *bon vivant* who knew which were the best vintage wines, what were the *spécialités de la maison* of famous restaurants, and where to find the right tailor; who liked to spend weekends with his socialite friends in the right places—mostly at Southampton or East Hampton on Long Island; and who, most of all, had an inordinate capacity to enjoy himself.

His greatest pleasure came from amusing his friends with his comic songs. This was the main reason why, one year, he was voted "the most entertaining man in his class." All of his songs had a satiric edge as sharp as a razor blade. One comic ballad which his fellow students liked particularly was "Miss Antoinette Birby," detailing the adventures of the heroine at the all-male Yale.

Porter became the leader of the college glee club. He also was involved in several other extracurricular activities devoted to either music or the stage. With Gerald Murphy he helped produce several college shows, one of them being *Robin Hood*. They also arranged a delectable evening of Elizabethan music for the school's cognoscenti. In addition to all this, Porter wrote college football songs. Two became famous and are still remembered: "Bingo Eli Yale" and "Bulldog," both of which were copyrighted in 1911. He also saw his first commercial song published—"Bridget," copyrighted on June 14, 1910, and issued a year later by the Tin Pan Alley firm of Jerome H. Remick.

AFTER BEING GRADUATED from Yale in 1913, Cole Porter yielded to his grandfather's wishes and entered law school—at Harvard. His roommate there was Dean Acheson, who was to become Secretary of State in the Cabinets of Presidents Franklin Delano Roosevelt and Harry Truman.

All the time that Porter was fussing over his law books, which he detested, his mind kept wandering off into versification and composition. He was no law scholar in the making. This truth, apparent to him in his very first weeks at Harvard, was also recognized by Ezra Ripley Thayer, Dean of the Law School. One day, Dean Thayer summoned Porter to his office. "Destiny," he told the young man, "intended you for music and not for law, and the fates must not be denied." He urged Porter to consider transferring without further delay from Harvard's Law School to its School of Music.

Cole, of course, approved heartily, but convincing his grandfather was something else again. In a stormy session in Peru, the old man made it clear that under no circumstances would he permit Cole to exchange law for music. "Tinkle the piano if you wish, and make up your pretty tunes if you must," bellowed the old man. "But don't try to make a career out of it." The old man dotted the "i's" and crossed the "t's", pointing out that those tunes would never pay the bills for the kind of life to which Cole had become accustomed. Besides, he asked gruffly, if Cole did not prepare himself for the job, who in the world would take over the running of the family interests once the two older men—Cole's grandfather and father—were no longer around to do so? "No," he insisted, "you must go back to law, and leave music to the birds."

Fortunately for Cole, he had a staunch ally in his mother, J. O. Cole's only child. In the face of Kate's pleas and arguments the old man was helpless. "All right," he finally told his daughter, "if that's the way you want it, that's the way it will have to be." The old man gave Cole his blessing, promised to continue his financial support, and in time the business interests were supervised by Cole's cousin.

At the School of Music, where Porter stayed three years, he received his first intensive education in areas outside playing an instrument—theory, counterpoint, music history, ear training, and so forth. This was the kind of all-embracing musical education which the School gave young men bent upon careers as serious composers, conductors, or virtuosos—young men like Leonard Bernstein who attended the Harvard School of Music in a later decade. But even while mastering the techniques needed by a serious musician, Cole Porter never harbored the ambition to write symphonies or operas, nor did he aspire to enter the concert world as a piano virtuoso. His all-consuming ambition was to write popular songs, but popular songs with a difference.

Porter had little interest in most of the songs then being published and popularized. The popular-song industry, known at that time as Tin Pan Alley, was actually named after a street in New York—Twenty-eighth Street between Fifth Avenue and Broadway, where an unusual concentration of music publishers could be found. But Tin Pan Alley was more than just a place where publishers had their offices. It stood for a way of life for American popular songs—a way of writing them to measure for specific performers and occasions; a way of merchandising them; a way of "plugging" them to success in theaters, restaurants, department and five-and-ten-cent stores. Year after year, Tin Pan Alley —like some giant factory—ground out songs in voluminous quantities and, through salesman and song pluggers, sold millions of copies in sheet music: sentimental ballads about rose-covered cottages, mother, the Southland, and frustrated love with which silver-toned Irish tenors and sobbing female torch singers brought down the house in vaudeville and on Broadway; ragtime tunes in syncopation and ingenuous waltzes in three-quarter time; nostalgic songs or humorous songs about the Irish. "Daddy Has a Sweetheart and Mother Is Her Name" . . . "When Irish Eyes Are Smiling" . . . "Let Me Call You Sweetheart," . . . "The Little Gray Home in the West" . . . "I Want a Girl Just Like the Girl That Married Dear Old Dad". . . . "Everybody's Doin' It"—to name a few.

One song after another followed simple, basic melodic patterns and formulas from which few ever dared to deviate. Too often the lyrics abounded with stilted rhymes and rhythms, clichés and bromides, bad grammar and worse prosody.

The kind of song Porter liked to write was partial to the novel, the unexpected, the surprising—both in lyrics and music. He enjoyed having his melody leap to an interval that caught the ear by surprise, and having that melody expand opulently beyond the limits of the thirty-two bars to which choruses were then confined. He liked to write his verses with tongue in cheek—humorous, sardonic, perhaps malicious verses, but all with a fresh point of view.

Other young ambitious song writers in the second decade of the century found their idols in Tin Pan Alley: in Ernest R. Ball, the greatest of the Irish balladeers; in Irving Berlin, king of ragtime; in Victor Herbert, the crown prince of American operetta. Cole Porter went elsewhere for a model and an inspiration—in fact, across the ocean to England—to Gilbert and Sullivan, geniuses of comic opera. His ambition was to become an *American* Gilbert and Sullivan, all by himself.

But at the time neither Tin Pan Alley nor Broadway seemed ready for an American Gilbert and Sullivan. Every attempt by Porter to invade the commercial market was doomed to failure. The Tin Pan Alley publishers called him highfalutin, saying that there just was no public for his kind of originality, wit, and cynicism. Broadway also rejected him soundly—but not without first giving him a hearing.

This hearing occurred in 1916.

While still attending the School of Music at Harvard, Cole Porter joined with his former fellow student at Yale, T. Lawrason Riggs, in writing a musical comedy. Riggs did the text, Porter, the lyrics and music. They called their brain child *See America First.* Elizabeth Marbury, a producer whom Porter had met in East Hampton, Long Island, became interested in the project and decided to mount it on Broadway, where she had recently enjoyed success with a fresh and sparkling little musical comedy called *Very Good, Eddie,* with music by Jerome Kern. This success had made her more receptive than usual to anything that was a little different from the ordinary run of Broadway musicals. She liked the dash and verve of Porter's lyrics and melodies, and she thought Riggs's satire in his dialogue and situations delightful.

Unfortunately, *See America First* was no *Very Good, Eddie*. With Clifton Webb (later a star of musical comedy and movies) as the leading performer, *See America First* opened at the Maxine Elliott Theatre on March 26, 1916. It lasted only fifteen performances. It was, truth to tell, pretty much of a bore. Stepping out from the script into the full and merciless glare of the theater limelight, the situations proved contrived, most of the humor fell flat, and many of the songs lacked popular appeal. Described in the program as a "patriotic comic opera," *See America First* was a take-off on the kind of flag-waving and chauvinistic George M. Cohan musical comedies, which made popular such songs as "Yankee Doodle Boy" and "You're a Grand Old Flag." *See America First* has for its main character an American who so detests foreigners that he makes it his life's work to prevent his daughter from marrying one. She, however, meets and falls in love with a titled Englishman, and in time our American reconciles himself to this development while beginning to lose his prejudice for those of foreign birth.

Here is how the *Dramatic Mirror* commented on Porter's songs: "The lyrics are studiously copied after the W. S. Gilbertian pattern with long complicated rhythmic effects. The music, however, gives the impression that its composer, after the first half hour, gave up the task of recreating a Gilbert and Sullivan atmosphere, preferring to seek his inspiration in our own George M. Cohan."

Only one song gave a hint of the later Cole Porter, a number called "I've Got a Shooting Box in Scotland."

None of the critics, however, noticed it within the context of the musical comedy. But Fred and Adele Astaire, the singing and dancing stars of vaudeville and musical comedy, liked it enough to use it in their vaudeville act. This song is still remembered fondly by Cole Porter admirers.

Soon after *See America First* had closed down, Cole Porter was invited to a party at the home of a New York socialite. The guests were all of the Social Register, and many of them had long known Cole Porter. Nevertheless, as he made his way from one group to another, he could tell that they were all talking about his recent Broadway disaster. He noticed how they tried to hide their snickers and suppress whispers as he approached, how overly effusive some were when they greeted him, how painful was the way in which some avoided talking about his show. In spite of these reactions—perhaps *because* of them—he jumped at the chance to play and sing some of his songs when invited to do so. He sang one number after another for an hour. "Cole is simply wonderful in the *salon*," someone remarked. "Too bad he is so awful in the theater."

A stout, dark-haired lady came to him when his performance had ended. Cole Porter recognized her—for she was the darling of the *haut monde*, the friend of European royalty, the giver of parties without an equal.

"Young man," she told him with the grand manner of a queen bestowing favors, "the only reason you are a failure on Broadway is because you are much too good.

Your standards are too high, while those of Tin Pan Alley are too low. The wit and poetry of your lyrics are far beyond them. But, mark well my words. One day you will haul the public to your own level, and then the world will be yours. And always remember that the first one to tell you so was Elsa Maxwell."

COLE PORTER ONCE EXPLAINED to a newspaper interviewer (more with good humor than bitterness) that the fiasco of *See America First* sent his librettist, T. Lawrason Riggs, to the priesthood, and himself to the French Foreign Legion. He added, "I had to leave town until the smell of my first Broadway show had disappeared."

But the compulsion to leave town came from a force other than failure. Having completed his music studies at Harvard in 1916, Porter heard the siren call of adventure. He wanted to see the world, not as a formal tourist this time, but as the hero of some dangerous escapade—and in an excitingly exotic setting. With the bravado of a character from a third-rate silent movie he joined the French Foreign Legion.

Unfortunately Fate was grooming him for a starring role in the live production soon to be known as the "roaring twenties." He was intended to be a playboy, not the dramatic hero in a glorious adventure. As a member of the French Foreign Legion in Africa, he did a good deal of marching. At times he was called upon to carry out some innocuous staff assignments. And that was all. Blood-curdling life-and-death struggles between Legionnaires and tribesmen, such as he had seen in the movies, remained, as far as he himself was concerned, fiction pure and simple.

While serving in the Legion, Porter carried on his back, together with the necessary military equipment, a portable piano which one of his friends from Philadelphia had given him just before he had enlisted. During hours freed from military preoccupations, Porter played and sang for the Legionnaires songs of his own invention, many of them inspired by his comrades-in-arms, and some by incidents in their daily routine. When, therefore, a grateful French Government bestowed on Porter the *Croix de guerre*—one of its most coveted military honors—it was not for bravery in action, of which he saw practically nothing, but because his personality, comradeship, and entertainments had helped to keep high the morale of his fellow Legionnaires.

Even when World War I broke out in Europe, the

danger and drama of conflict seemed to elude Porter. Wearing the sky-blue uniform of the French army, he served far back of the fighting lines. In fact most of his time was spent at the French Officers' School in Fontainebleau. During leaves, he attended all kinds of gay parties in Paris, none of which lost any of their glamour or ebullient gaiety because of the war.

With America's entry into the conflict, Porter was assigned to teach French gunnery to American soldiers. Thus once again he was removed from the pale of danger and, military duties notwithstanding, was afforded frequent opportunities to entertain the social and military elite in a beautifully appointed and spacious apartment he had rented in Paris. He also found the time to continue writing songs. One of them, completed within the sound of German cannon booming toward Paris, was "Old-Fashioned Garden," which later became his first commercial hit.

The war ended without inflicting any visible scars on Porter; also without giving him any specific direction as to a career or a definite purpose in life.

He was a guest at a wedding at the Ritz Hotel in Paris when he was introduced to Linda Lee Thomas. She was a former Louisville, Kentucky, belle—a young woman of striking beauty and surpassing charm. She had been married to and recently divorced from E. R. Thomas, a successful and prominent American newspaper owner. A single meeting between her and Porter was enough to convince each that they had one very important thing in common—the love of life. They responded to each other instinctively and immediately and romantic interest developed rapidly. Porter knew that this was the woman he wanted to make his wife, but before venturing on matrimony, he decided to go home to seek his grandfather's blessing.

Late in 1919, Porter was back in his native city. The ensuing conference proved explosive. The old man—bitterly disappointed that Cole had not become a lawyer or exhibited any readiness to take over the family business—denounced his grandson's aimless and irresponsible ways. Highhandedly he dismissed all of Porter's creative efforts as only so much "hogwash"—certainly no way for a respectable man of high financial and social status to spend his working hours. As for marrying a divorced woman (even if she was in the Social Register) and settling permanently with her in Paris—this, as far as J. O. Cole was concerned, was out of the question. He sternly and firmly announced that he would—if Cole married Linda—wash his hands clean once and for all of his prodigal grandson.

Porter went back to Paris without his grandfather's good wishes—but with no weakening of his determination to marry the woman he loved. Soon after his return, in December of 1919, Cole Porter and Linda Lee Thomas were quietly married in a civil ceremony in the office of the local *Mairie* (Mayor). Since Linda Lee was a person of means—and since Porter was being handsomely supported by his parents—they were able to set up an elegantly furnished apartment on the Rue Monsieur, and to make it one of the most fashionable and exciting salons in Paris.

If Porter had been unable to gain his grandfather's blessing during his brief visit home, the trip was not without accompanying rewards. En route to the United States, aboard ship, Porter had met Raymond Hitchcock, a well-known musical comedy star then producing on Broadway an annual revue called *Hitchy-Koo*. Porter played some of his songs for Hitchcock. "Old-Fashioned Garden" struck Hitchcock's fancy particularly. He contracted with Porter to write the score for the next edition of the revue. This was to be Porter's first return to the Broadway scene after the 1916 disaster of *See America First*.

That return took place on October 6, 1919, at the Liberty Theater, with *Hitchy-Koo of 1919*, whose principal performers included Raymond Hitchcock, Joe Cook, Lillian Kemble Cooper, and Florence O'Denishawn. Porter contributed ten songs, among them an amusing duet, "When I Had a Uniform", shared by Joe Cook and Eleanor Sinclair. Several others were introduced by Hitchcock, the best being one of Porter's earliest commercial songs about Paris, "My Cozy Little Corner in the Ritz."

The hit song of the production was "Old-Fashioned Garden" which Hitchcock had insisted go into the score, and which was delightfully presented by Lillian Kemble Cooper. There were suggestions of the later Porter in the infectious way in which melody and lyric, hand in hand, tripped lightly down the path of sophistication. The audience was enchanted: the song stopped the show regularly both on Broadway and on the road. The sheet-music sale of over one hundred thousand copies brought its composer his first impressive returns as song writer—royalties in excess of $10,000.

"It was my first hit," Porter has said about this number, "and it is still one of my favorites." In fact, he saw to it that the song was revived in his motion-picture biography *Night and Day* when it was being filmed in the nineteen-forties.

THE PORTERS' FIRST "OPEN HOUSE" in their swank new Paris apartment coincided with the birth of the nineteen-twenties. For the next decade Cole and Linda Porter reflected the feverish, extravagant, often reckless mood of the times. They *belonged* to the twenties. They *were* the twenties. For them life was to be a continual "trip to the moon on gossamer wings" (to borrow a line from one of Porter's later songs).

In the twenties, a good many Americans thought it

was the height of maturity, culture, and *savoir-faire* to live as expatriates in Paris—a city free and open in its tolerance, gracious toward artists and Bohemians, fully appreciative not only of the arts but also of the subtleties and refinements of good living. This was the city which was regarded as home by such American writers as F. Scott Fitzgerald, Ernest Hemingway, Gertrude Stein, Sherwood Anderson—the vanguard of a literary invasion of France from the United States. The salon and the café became for them a source of literary stimulation and the setting for good conversation. This was the city where such then avant-garde American composers as George Antheil and Aaron Copland could write as outlandishly as they pleased and find appreciative ears. The Porters were among the earliest of these post-World War I expatriates. To them Paris was a setting as natural as platinum is to diamond. And they did their best to set the tone for a decade that would be spinning to the strains of a hectic tune.

Their parties, crowded with celebrities, were the last word in lavishness. They became even more grandiose after 1923 when J. O. Cole, died and (in spite of his earlier threat) left his grandson a million dollars. The Porters acquired a $250,000 mansion in the exclusive Faubourg St. Germain section where zebra-skin upholstery, kid-skin chairs, rooms decorated in platinum leaf, and floor-to-ceiling opaque mirrors all contributed to an air of opulence. "Their house in Paris," the playwright, Moss Hart, has written, "was one of the most beautiful I have ever seen."

Much of the elegance, however, was just a reflection of the personalities of the hosts. Cole Porter was the man of the world who kept an alert finger on the pulse of everything that was anything, and everyone who was anyone in Paris' social and cultural life. He was a man who accepted luxury as his due.

Many years later, Lucius Beebe, the famous society columnist, would say of Porter, with a generous dash of irony: "It is really the *simple* things of life that gave pleasure to Mr. Porter. Half-million-dollar strings of pearls, Isotta motor cars, cases of double bottles of Grand Chambertin '87, suites at Claridge's, brief trips aboard the *Bremen*, a little grouse shooting. . . . He is on all the first-night lists, Leon at L'Aperitif salutes him as 'Highness,' he is reputed to travel with his own linen sheets, punkah wavers, court chamberlains, and sauce cooks."

Lucius Beebe might have written the same way of Porter in the nineteen-twenties, had he known him at that time. Then, as later, Porter was the model of sartorial elegance—a foppish boutonniere in his lapel an indispensable part of his wardrobe. Then, as later, he was a man of uncommon grace and wit, whose conversations were as clever as many of the songs he devised for the delectation of his friends and guests.

And Linda Lee proved a worthy partner. "A legendary beauty," wrote Moss Hart, "[she] lent something of her own radiance and splendor to their life, so that everything and everyone in their house seemed to sparkle with a little of her grace. She was a woman of immense delicacy, as easily beguiled by a chorus girl as by a duchess, and equally at home with both."

The cream of European society, culture, and politics (sometimes numbering hundreds at one time) could be found regularly at the Porters'—people like the Prince of Wales (destined to renounce the throne of England for the woman he loved); the Princess de Polignac, a leading figure in Parisian *haut monde;* Cecil Beaton, the famous British photographer; Noel Coward, the brilliant Jack-of-all-trades in the London theater; Monty Woolley, the actor; and Elsa Maxwell, who had become one of the Porters' closest friends. Titled people, stars of the entertainment world, gifted representatives of the arts, people who wielded immense political or financial power—all rubbed elbows with each other. Two or three dozen footmen would attend to the needs of the guests. Sometimes the parties were enlivened with performances by such world-famous musicians as Maurice Ravel or Igor Stravinsky. Sometimes they were brightened by new songs written for the occasion by Cole Porter or Noel Coward. At one time, the whole troupe of Diaghilev's world-famous Ballet Russe came to a Cole Porter party to present *Les Sylphides.* No expense was spared to make one party or ball more lavish and more talked about than its predecessor. At one of their fancy balls, the Porters themselves provided the costumes for six hundred guests!

When a dance called the Charleston became the rage, first in America and then in Paris, the Porters held Charleston parties three times a week. An unknown chanteuse called Bricktop was hired to teach the guests the intricate body motions and steps of the dance. Cole Porter had seen her perform one evening in a Paris night spot in 1925 and had been delighted with her talent and personal appeal. She, too, was an American expatriate, who would in time become one of Paris' most celebrated night-club stars.

These parties might last through a night—sometimes they stretched on for days. They were given not only in Paris but also in London. There were times when the Porters transported their many friends and special guests from Paris to Cannes on the French Riviera or to the Lido in Venice by special trains, or in motorcades headed by their own Rolls Royce. When traveling by themselves, the Porters required no less than nine train compartments to accommodate their valet and maid, and to provide a bar, a sitting room, and sleeping quarters.

The thousand and one nights in Venice, each more splendiferous than the one before, began in 1923 when the Porters rented the Palazzo Barbaro at the Lido. For four seasons, beginning with 1925, they took over the Palazzo Rezzonico where Robert Browning, the great English poet, had died; this place cost the Porters a thousand dollars a week to run. The balls in these sumptuous surroundings were the talk of Venice. Diversions ranged from the unusual to the quixotic: a treasure hunt through the canals, for example. One night, a troupe of tightrope walkers were the entertainers; on another, fifty gondoliers served as footmen. The Porters eventually built a night club alongside the canal, accommodating one hundred and fifty diners and featuring a French chef and either a Negro jazz band or a string orchestra.

The Porters were always on the move, for the age was a restless one. Besides their house in Paris and their rented palaces in Venice, they owned a villa in Bavaria. They thought little of going to Morocco for a few days or, at the whim of a moment, setting off for some such exotic place as Bali, in one part of the globe, or Haiti, in another. Wherever they went, they transported the spirit of the twenties with them. Festivities whirled around them like the colors of a vividly decorated spinning top.

In the twenties a wisecrack was looked upon as the cream of wisdom as well as jest, with Dorothy Parker the high priestess of the cult. The twenties saw infinite effort, ingenuity, and resources expended on the perpetration of a prank. Playing jokes on one another was a cherished pastime of the Porter set.

At one gala affair, Monty Woolley (already sporting a handsome beard) arrived with a beautifully groomed young lady. She was also bearded! Woolley behaved with the quiet nonchalance of a gentleman long accustomed to escorting bearded ladies to parties. But a prank that really sent Paris society spinning on its ear was one Cole Porter himself pulled off. In 1925, he created out of thin air a couple whom he called Mr. and Mrs. Fitch. He explained that they were wealthy Americans from a little town called Muskogee, and that they were being eagerly sought after by the most fashionable salons in Paris. Porter despatched an announcement to the Paris *Herald* that the Fitches were the guests of honor at a highly exclusive dinner given by Elsa Maxwell. He kept sending items about the Fitches to the social columns of that paper: their presence at the Longchamps race track, or at this or that fashionable restaurant; their late arrival at the opera; their early departure from a ball at this or that Embassy.

Everybody in Paris soon came to know the Fitches by name, discussed the places where they had last been seen. When several Parisian socialites started boasting to envious friends that the Fitches had been guests at their dinner parties, Porter's delight knew no limits. The hoax lasted until one of the editors of the *Herald* became aware that the Fitches were figments of Porter's imagination. Recognizing how this business would embarrass his society columnist, the editor inserted a news item to the effect that the Fitches had been killed in an auto accident in Italy.

However much Cole Porter enjoyed all these delightful escapades, however naturally he fitted into the sumptuous night life of Paris and Venice, he was nevertheless beginning to search for some goal in life other than laughing and carousing. He was seeking for an identity as a cultured man, as a creator. Of course, what he wanted most of all to do was to write songs, but except for his own circle there seemed to be no audience for the kind of material that came to him so naturally.

In the first half of the twenties, he had made two new attempts to invade the American musical theater. Raymond Hitchcock had asked him to contribute several numbers to the *Hitchy-Koo of 1922*, which he did. But that show had collapsed in Boston before coming to New York, and the six numbers Cole Porter composed for it passed on to oblivion. In 1924 he had written five songs for the *Greenwich Village Follies*. There the Dolly Sisters sang "I'm in Love Again;" Georgie Hale presented a nostalgic number about Brittany, and George Rasely lent his dulcet tenor tones to "My Long-Ago Girls." But none of these Porter songs had made any kind of an impression on the theatergoing public.

Since recognition seemed so far away, Cole Porter decided to go back to music school. He enrolled in the renowned Schola Cantorum in Paris where he studied composition under Vincent d'Indy, one of France's most highly esteemed composers. At the same time, Porter began to dabble with paints. For a while—in despair of ever making any headway in the theater—he thought seriously of devoting himself more conscientiously to art than to song writing.

Of course, all the while he also kept on giving, and going to, those fabulous parties; he kept on playing games and pranks; he kept on enjoying culinary specialties and imbibing choice vintage champagnes; he kept on traveling; he kept on making those "crazy flings" and those "fabulous flights." After all, the twenties were now in high gear.

WHILE COLE PORTER was disporting in the playgrounds of Europe, and while he was creating his own brand of popular song, the song-writing and musical-comedy standards in America were changing rapidly. A decade that liked to make a fetish of smart and sophisticated attitudes, of satirical approaches, and of rapier-edged wit, provided the climate in which brave new creative personalities could emerge, be heard, and be appreciated. Such composers as Jerome Kern, George Gershwin, and Richard Rodgers were bringing to composition a freshness of style, an infectiousness of spirit, and a variety of invention heretofore rarely encountered either on Broadway or in Tin Pan Alley. These men tapped new veins in the writing of popular songs. They made full use of the resources of harmony and rhythm to enrich and vary the direction of the melodic line. They were frequently ready to break down the long-accepted rule that in a popular song the verse should be in sixteen measures and the chorus in thirty-two; they allowed their lyrical ideas to acquire more *Lebensraum*—space to move about—through a more expansive structure. At the same time Lorenz Hart and Ira Gershwin, among other lyricists, were finally ridding song lyrics of their platitudes, their infantile versification, their sophomoric ways of expressing emotion. The old flotsams and jetsams of lyric writing were cast aside for colorful imagery, virtuoso techniques, and the rich spices of mockery, malice, and irony.

Musical comedies and revues were presenting slicker stage methods, more adult subject matter, more American and contemporary setting and situation, and more colloquial speech. The result was that those homespun productions—like the musical comedies of George M. Cohan—that had captured the hearts of theatergoers, during the first decade of the nineteen-hundreds, had become in the nineteen-twenties as old-fashioned as the surrey with the fringe on top. The twenties were a new age for American popular music and for the American musical theater, an age when a fresh creative spirit like that of Cole Porter could come into its own.

Porter, of course, was increasingly aware of the new scheme of things developing in Tin Pan Alley and on Broadway. That he had a place in it did not, however, become apparent to him until the latter half of the decade, when he met E. Ray Goetz at the Lido in Venice. Goetz was a Broadway producer who—in tune with the times—was planning an urbane musical comedy set in Paris to star the Parisian musical-comedy favorite, Irene Bordoni, who happened to be, in private life, Mrs. E. Ray Goetz. The name of this new musical was to be simply *Paris*. Goetz revealed some of the ideas he had for this show, and Porter responded enthusiastically. Goetz said he needed songs suitable for such a frame, songs that would have the piquant flavor of Parisian life and mores and points of view. He insisted that none of the successful Broadway composers and lyricists were up to such a task, since it called for someone who had some of Paris in his blood.

"What I'm thinking of, Cole," Goetz concluded, "is that you are the man for the job. The kind of songs I've heard you sing at your parties are the kind of songs I'd like to see in a show like *Paris*."

Now free to write for Broadway exactly as he pleased, Porter completed eight numbers, of which five were finally used. The text and setting of *Paris* permitted him to indulge in his natural flair for leaping rhymes and rhythms, for cultured allusions of all sorts, for mischievous *double-entendres*. One such number was the still-familiar "Let's Do It." The lilting, sparkling but by no means iconoclastic tune served the words most admirably, although in itself it was nothing exceptional. The words, however, introduced into the Broadway theater, and into popular song, a sparkle and a sheen and a chuckle that henceforth would ever identify Porter. With the added spice of Irene Bordoni's piquant French accent, this was a dish that the sophisticate of the twenties could relish. This was a far cry from the old "June-moon" kind of rhyming, and the "I love you, I love you, is all that I can say," kind of romancing by which the popular song had so long been identified. (In 1960, "Let's Do It" was used in a parody as a beer commercial over radio and TV.)

There were other equally inviting numbers in that score. One, very much in the saucy manner of "Let's Do It" was "Let's Misbehave." Unfortunately, at the out-of-town tryout, the director found that this song slowed up the action and insisted that it be dropped. Never used in the show, but issued as an independent number, "Let's Misbehave" became one of Cole Porter's most popular creations of the late nineteen-twenties.

There were two other Cole Porter songs in the show that were decided assets to it, both of them written for and made memorable by Irene Bordoni: "Two Little Babes in the Wood" and "Don't Look at Me That Way." Cole Porter's songs and Irene Bordoni's performance helped make *Paris* a success, though a minor one, when it opened in New York at the Music Box Theatre on October 8, 1928.

The favorable reaction of audiences and critics to Cole Porter's contribution to *Paris* led to an immediate renewal of the collaboration between composer and producer. E. Ray Goetz decided to do another musical comedy with a Parisian background. He recruited Herbert Fields to write the text, and thus began a working partnership between Herbert Fields and Cole Porter that yielded several outstanding box-office triumphs in the nineteen-thirties.

Herbert Fields came from a theatrical family; the stage was in his blood. His father was Lew Fields, the comedian who had made theatrical history as part of the team of Weber and Fields and then had gone on to become a famous Broadway star and producer. Herbert's brother, Joseph, achieved renown as a musical-comedy librettist and playwright; their sister, Dorothy, made a shining name for herself as a lyricist.

Herbert Fields's entry into the theater came by way of bit parts in several plays. From acting he turned to writing. As the collaborator of Lorenz Hart and Richard Rodgers, he was responsible for producing some of the brightest, most unusual musical-comedy texts of the twenties, notably *Dearest Enemy* in 1925, *Peggy Ann* in 1926, and *A Connecticut Yankee* in 1927. He was, then, one of Broadway's most successful librettists when Goetz called him in to write a Parisian musical comedy with Cole Porter's songs.

As *Fifty Million Frenchmen*—with a cast headed by William Gaxton and Genevieve Tobin—this new Herbert Fields-Cole Porter musical comedy opened in

New York at the Lyric Theatre on November 27, 1929. It stayed there for 254 performances, which in the twenties represented a solid hit.

Fifty Million Frenchmen was even more Parisian than *Paris* had been. Fields's text "covered the wondrous city of the Seine with seven-league boots," as I explained in the *Complete Book of the American Musical Theater*, "from the Ritz bar to the Longchamps race track; from the American Express Company on Rue Scribe to Montmartre; from the Claridge Hotel to Les Halles. En route, it gently spoofed American tourists."

One of the American tourists in the musical is the wealthy playboy, Peter Forbes; another is Looloo, a girl from Terre Haute, with whom he has fallen in love. Determined to win Looloo's love, not for his money but for himself alone, Peter decides to pose as a pauper. He fills various menial jobs to support himself, including those of a guide, a gigolo, and a fake Arabian magician. During his many and varied experiences on the boulevards and in the alleys of Paris he continually crosses paths with Looloo, who is being hotly pursued all the while by a Grand Duke. In time, Looloo begins to respond more and more enthusiastically to this young "impoverished" American. Peter wins her, after becoming convinced that it is for himself alone that she has learned to love him.

For this lively libretto, Cole Porter created his finest score up to this time. Indeed, it stands up well even against some of his later, more successful accomplishments. Drawing deeply on his own experiences in

Paris—along its boulevards, in its cafés and boîtes—Porter for the first time commercially achieved identity as a composer and lyricist. "Find Me a Primitive Man," "You've Got That Thing," and "You Do Something to Me" are so much in his most intriguing, most irresistible, and most personal sardonic, tongue-in-the-cheek style that they truly can be said to have ushered in the Cole Porter era in American musical comedy and American popular song. "You Do Something to Me" particularly is top-drawer Porter both in music and in words. The way in which, midway in the chorus, the melody begins its ecstatic flight; the way in which, in the same release, interior rhymes trip along nimbly one after another ("*do* do, the *voo*doo, that *you* do so well")—all this pinpoints the fact that Porter's distinctive creative talents were beginning to unfold.

Two other numbers sang the praises of Paris, a subject which henceforth would be calculated to spark his creative impulses. "You Don't Know Paree" and "Paree, What You Did to Me" were full of that haunting nostalgia, on the one hand, and Gallic sparkle on the other, which always carried over into Porter's song writing whenever he spoke about the city of light.

The critics listened to these songs, became aware for the first time they were in the presence of a master, and let loose with superlatives. Robert Littell in the New York *World*, called "Find Me a Primitive Man" "one of the best pieces of popular music I have ever heard." He added: "Mr. Porter has given the show many other good tunes. 'You've Got That Thing,' with a remarkable piano part, is certainly one of them with far, far better words than are usually to be found in musical comedy."

Richard Watts, Jr., in the *Herald Tribune*, called *Fifty Million Frenchmen* "pretty much of a Cole Porter field day and, because he is a master of his profession, the show is a striking one."

John Mason Brown, in the *Evening Post*, said: "The music is of such a kind that it makes sitting still next to impossible."

One of the most astute and discriminating of all the critics, George Jean Nathan, and one hardest to please, wrote in a magazine piece: "When it comes to lyrics, this Cole Porter is so far ahead of the other boys in New York that there just is no race."

Cole Porter's creative personality continued to unfold in two more songs which were written before the twenties drew to a close. One was "What Is This Thing Called Love?" which Frances Shelley introduced in *Wake Up and Dream*, a second Cole Porter musical comedy reaching Broadway in 1929. The other was "Love for Sale," sung by Kathryn Crawford in *The New Yorkers*, the Cole Porter musical comedy of 1930. Each of these productions would long since have been forgotten (neither one was a box-office success) but for the fact that they gave birth to these two song classics. The qualities that would identify Porter's greatest songs are here fully realized: the often minor-key, Slavic kind of melody that sweeps relentlessly toward an exciting climax—often over an irresistible rhythm; the lyrics abounding with sophisticated allusions, made provocative and suggestive through *double-entendres*, and always fashioned with the most breath-taking virtuosity in the use of rhyme and rhythm.

Act Two
The Sober Thirties

that had been the twenties was over. The stock-market collapse in October of 1929 was followed by a disastrous economic depression. Business crumbled. Life savings melted away. Jobs became scarce. Hotels, theaters, restaurants were empty. Bread lines and soup kitchens were hurriedly improvised to feed the swelling army of the unemployed. Shanty towns sprang up on vacant lots to provide housing for those no longer able to pay rent. The winter of discontent was at hand. Labor was coming to serious grips with management. Strikes spread like contagion. A bedraggled army of World War I veterans began a march to Washington, and the militia had to be called out to disperse it. A generation that had once sung "Ain't We Got Fun?" was now chanting "Brother, Can You Spare a Dime?" and "In a Shanty in Old Shanty Town."

The intoxication of the twenties was over; only the hangover remained. Having a good time at any price, with a quip on the lips and a devil-may-care philosophy in the heart, had lost its one-time fascination. Sobriety was setting in. People were becoming acutely conscious of social and political problems; a healthier set of values began to take hold.

The expatriates were coming home. Cole Porter and his wife came with them. Paris was no longer as much fun as it had been. The glow and glitter of its life had become dulled by the somber realities of the economic crisis; the gaiety and frivolity of the twenties had become synthetic and forced. But for Cole Porter's homecoming there was an even stronger reason than the change in the social and emotional climate. By 1930, largely because of *Fifty Million Frenchmen* and songs like "You Do Something to Me" and "What Is This Thing Called Love?", Porter had become Broadway's new shining light. Demands on his services were coming thick and fast. His career, now that he was successful, assumed first place in his life. Developing that career further—and producing songs to ensure that development—was of far greater concern than having a good time, and it demanded that he establish a base close to the Great White Way—Broadway—if he was to function to his fullest creative capacity. Songs always had to be rewritten and new ones devised while a show was in rehearsal, or during out-of-town tryouts. Doing such chores long distance was difficult, if not impossible. In addition, Porter felt the need to be close at hand during rehearsal time to be sure that his songs were being properly sung and presented. With his musical comedies now a part of the Broadway scene every season, his presence in New York for extended periods every year became a necessity. The time had come, the Porters finally decided, to make the move permanent, to set up a new home for themselves in New York City.

Financially, they were not affected by the Depression, and for this reason they were among the rare few able to carry the spirit of the twenties into the thirties. Their zest for good times, their passion for travel, their fetish for elegance remained undiminished. The holiday for Porter was by no means over, but now it came, as it should, after periods of intensive work. Life for him would henceforth combine play with the driving, indefatigable business of getting on paper the best possible melodies and verses, serving one Broadway show after another. Exhilaration, excitement, the rise of pulse and heartbeat, the tingling of the senses—all these now came not only from a new variation on the theme of gay living but also from a creative job well done.

In the twenties, Cole Porter's caricature had worn a

single face, that of playboy. In the thirties it had two, for the playboy could also be a fastidious workman. Moss Hart, who collaborated with Porter in the early thirties, put it this way: "Cole is the most self-indulgent and pleasure-loving man I have ever known; but indulgence and pleasure stop dead the moment songwriting begins."

DURING THE THIRTIES, Cole Porter wrote over a hundred songs for eight Broadway musicals, and original scores for three Hollywood motion pictures. At least a dozen of these songs are among his greatest, and their survival in the repertory of American popular music seems assured.

He went from one assignment to the next, with the ink hardly dry on the preceding manuscript. The creative urge, fully released by his first successes, could be denied no longer. He wrote because he had to write; because his ideas for music and verse would give him no peace until they were committed to paper. And he wrote copiously.

His first stage success in the nineteen-thirties came with *The Gay Divorce*. This musical comedy, starring Fred Astaire, came to the Ethel Barrymore Theatre on November 29, 1932. The trivial plot concerned the efforts of Mimi, an actress, to get a divorce. For this purpose, Guy (played by Astaire) is hired to pose as co-respondent, and he does his job so well that the two fall in love. This was surely a slender thread on which to hang jewels, but apparently it served Cole Porter well. For one of these jewels, "Night and Day," is probably one of the greatest American popular songs ever written—a song significant enough among Porter's achievements to supply the title for his screen biography, released in 1946.

"Night and Day," sung by Fred Astaire and Claire Luce, then danced to by Astaire, stood out from its context like pure gold in the company of brass. In fact, the song was largely responsible for making *The Gay Divorce* a smashing box-office success. At first the show failed to attract interest, since the critics had been lukewarm to the thrice-familiar plot and the contrived characters and situations. But "Night and Day" was selling sheet music and phonograph records, and it was becoming a prime favorite with the big name bands throughout the country. Inevitably, the more "Night and Day" was heard—and by early 1933 it was heard everywhere over the radio—the more people became curious about the show of which it was a part. Business at the Ethel Barrymore Theatre started to pick up until sold-out houses became the rule. Throughout its run of almost 250 performances, *The Gay Divorce* was frequently referred to as "that 'Night and Day' show."

The hypnotic effect of the repeated B-flats in the verse had been suggested to Porter during one of his trips to exotic places—Morocco—where, from a distance, he heard the beating of a tom-tom. This helped to make "Night and Day" one of the most exciting original song creations of the nineteen-thirties; so did the refreshing release of the chorus which extended through forty-eight measures instead of the usual thirty-two. From Fred Astaire to Paul Whiteman and André Kostelanetz, from Bing Crosby to Benny Goodman, there was hardly a successful recording artist in the thirties—who did not bring his version to disks. A recording by the Tommy Dorsey Orchestra in the early nineteen-forties was one of Frank Sinatra's earliest disks, Sinatra then being the vocalist of the Dorsey band.

"Night and Day" also proved the big hit song in movies when *The Gay Divorce* was made into a delightful song-and-dance musical for Fred Astaire and Ginger Rogers. With the title altered only to the extent of an added "e" at the end of the word "divorce," the motion picture was released by RKO in 1934. However, in spite of the popularity and importance of "Night and Day" —and the spectacular way in which it was presented in the movie—it failed surprisingly to gain the highest honor the film industry could bestow on it. The Academy of Motion Picture Arts and Sciences decided that year to introduce a new category among its "Oscar" awards—one for popular songs. When the votes were counted, this coveted prize went not to "Night and Day" but to another number in *The Gay Divorcee*, and strange to say, to one *not* by Porter. For into his score there had been interpolated a new song, lyrics by Herb Magidson, music by Con Conrad. It was called "The Continental" and it served to inspire an exciting South-American dance creation for Fred Astaire and Ginger Rogers. And to "The Continental" went the distinction of being the first popular song to win the Academy Award.

Successful though *The Gay Divorce* had been on Broadway, it was completely outdistanced by the Cole Porter musical comedy that followed it immediately. *Anything Goes* opened at the Alvin Theatre on November 2, 1934 and became the longest-running Cole Porter musical in the thirties (420 performances). *Anything Goes* was topflight musical theatre, good enough to survive the nineteen-thirties and to become a lavish television spectacular in the nineteen-fifties; good enough to enjoy numerous revivals throughout the years both on the summer circuit and off Broadway; good enough to have not one but two successful motion-picture adaptations (the first in 1936 with Bing Crosby and Ethel Merman; the second, twenty years later, with Bing Crosby, Donald O'Connor, and Mitzi Gaynor). Reviewing the second motion-picture version in 1956, A. H. Weiler gave full measure to *Anything Goes* by saying in the New York *Times*: "Age has not withered this property."

Anything Goes had a strange history. The text, as

originally prepared by Guy Bolton and P. G. Wodehouse, concerned a shipwreck and its amusing effects on a bunch of screwball characters. However, just before *Anything Goes* went into production, a marine disaster hit the front pages: the ship, the *Morro Castle*, burst into flames off the coast of New Jersey, costing 134 lives. A shipwreck, obviously, could no longer serve as material for comedy. The text of *Anything Goes* had to be completely revamped. Since P. G. Wodehouse was then in London, and Guy Bolton in Paris, the producer (Vinton Freedley) asked Howard Lindsay and Russel Crouse to work out a new script.

Crouse had written a humorous column in the New York *Evening Post* between 1924 and 1929 and in 1932 had become the press agent for the New York Theatre Guild, producers of distinguished plays on a subscription basis. Howard Lindsay had achieved success as an actor in vaudeville, burlesque, silent films, and on the Broadway stage, before becoming an even more successful playwright. With the assignment to rewrite *Anything Goes* they became collaborators for the first time. This fact is of particular significance for the American theater —not only because *Anything Goes* was one of Cole Porter's finest musicals, but also because the team of Russel Crouse and Howard Lindsay went on to write other distinguished musical-comedy texts and also to make stage history, first with *Life With Father*, which enjoyed the longest run of any play in Broadway history, then with *State of the Union*, which received the Pulitzer Prize in 1946.

The shipwreck idea for *Anything Goes* was completely discarded. Instead, a luxury liner crossing the Atlantic from New York to Southampton was made part of the setting for a passenger list that included Public Enemy No. 13 disguised as a clergyman; a night-club singer turned evangelist; a stowaway playboy, concealing his identity through all kinds of amusing disguises as he follows the girl of his heart aboard ship. The rest of the scenes were laid in England where the various complications became neatly disentangled, and the playboy won the girl he was pursuing. At the same time Public Enemy No. 13 learned to his horror that Washington, D. C., considered him about as dangerous as a cream puff. "I can't understand this administration," was his whining comment.

One of the things that made *Anything Goes* a "thundering good song and dance show," as Brooks Atkinson described it in the New York *Times,* was the casting. Public Enemy No. 13, disguised as Reverend Moon, was one of Victor Moore's most unforgettable characterizations. He was a pathetic-faced, broken-voiced, timid, mild-mannered little man who liked to consider himself a public menace, though a zephyr would have been enough to throw him into a panic. The playboy, Billy Crocker, was portrayed by William Gaxton in a performance that was brash and full of bounce. And as Reno Sweeney, the night-club singer turned evangelist, Ethel Merman was at the top of her singing form. Her brassy delivery, that bounced Porter's songs off the topmost rafters of the theater like the piercing tones of Louis Armstrong's trumpet, added further distinction to several songs that rank high among Porter's all-time hits. One of these was "You're the Top", one of the best patter songs Porter ever wrote, full of urbane allusions to subjects ranging from a Bendel bonnet to a Shakespeare sonnet and from a symphony of Strauss to Mickey Mouse. Another was "Blow, Gabriel, Blow", a lusty ballad in the style of a revivalist hymn, tailor-made for Merman's metallic delivery. A third was "I Get a Kick Out of You."

When Porter first played "I Get a Kick Out of You" for Merman, she was skeptical as to whether or not she could do it justice. She said it lacked the kind of punch her songs needed. But, one day, during rehearsals, she took liberty with the word "terrifically" in the chorus. She broke it up into its several syllables, pausing for a moment on the syllable "rif." That little trick energized the number. As Merman herself explained, "it killed the people, and it helped make the song the hit of a show filled with outstanding musical numbers."

Its powerful effect on the audience was all the more remarkable in view of the fact that this number was placed early in the show—in fact, only three minutes after the rise of the first-act curtain. It is rare to introduce so important a song before an audience has had the chance to warm up to a show. But as Maurice Zolotow explained in *There's No Business Like Show Business*, Merman "knocked the audience, totally unprepared, for a 'loop.' " Russel Crouse told an interviewer that, after Merman's delivery of "I Get a Kick Out of You", she "just couldn't do anything wrong for that audience."

A FEW WEEKS AFTER the successful opening of *Anything Goes*, Porter was having lunch with Moss Hart, who was, by 1935, also a person of consequence in the theater. With George S. Kaufman he had written a rollicking satire on Hollywood, *Once in a Lifetime*. This play, produced in 1930, was Moss Hart's first Broadway production and his first box-office triumph. He later wrote brilliant texts for two outstanding musical comedies, both of them with

Irving Berlin—*Face the Music* in 1932 and *As Thousands Cheer* in 1933.

As invariably happens when two men of the theater are together, ideas for Broadway productions—and musical comedies specifically—were discussed. Moss Hart touched on a theme that at the moment intrigued him, a play about a royal family in exile. "But," he told Porter, "I'm afraid I'll let that lie for a while. I've set my heart on taking a trip around the world first. My next musical comedy will come after that."

Porter replied softly, "Why not kill two birds with one stone? Why not write your musical comedy and take your trip around the world? Take one of those leisurely several-month cruises, and work as you go."

Hart digested this suggestion for a silent moment.

Porter continued, "You know what, Moss. I like that theme of yours, and I'd like to work with you. Why can't we both take that trip around the world and at the same time write a musical comedy?"

Their enthusiasm kept mounting as they exchanged ideas on how the royal-family-in-exile theme could best be developed and what kind of songs would be suitable. And the idea of writing a musical comedy while circling the globe on a luxury liner grew increasingly inviting the more they contemplated it.

"No reason why the whole thing isn't practical," Porter insisted. "I'll tell you what, Moss. If the idea is as good as it sounds to us, Linda will be the first to tell us so. Let me call her and get her reaction."

Linda Lee Porter's reaction was most enthusiastic. It

would be wonderful to have Moss Hart write a libretto for her husband, since she regarded Hart as one of the most brilliant of the young playwrights. She thought that a cruise around the world would be an ideal way of combining hard work with relaxation. She urged her husband to go ahead with his plans immediately—before his enthusiasm and excitement simmered down.

"When would you be ready to leave with us, Linda?" Porter asked.

"Not *me*, not *us*, just you and Moss. You always work best without anybody around you, and I can only be a nuisance to you. Besides you know that when you're working you're impossible to live with. The best thing is for you and Moss to go off by yourselves, and come back with the musical comedy finished."

And that's the way it happened. Immediately after lunch, Porter and Hart made for a travel bureau to inquire for the first available world cruise. Then and there they booked passage on the *Franconia*, departing from New York on January 12, 1935.

The first ten days aboard ship were days of glorious leisure, of basking in the sun, sipping bouillon in the morning and cocktails in late afternoon, of gourmet meals and shipboard entertainment. But all the while some work was being done. The two kept talking all around the theme of their musical, trying to carry the plot to its logical conclusion, to fill in some of the humorous details.

The ship was making its way south toward tropical sun and skies. At Kingston, Jamaica, Porter became the indefatigable, insatiable tourist as was habitual with him whenever he came to an interesting place. He went from one end of the island to the other seeking out every possible point of interest, every native curiosity or peculiarity. "The flora and fauna fascinated him," Moss Hart later recalled, "and he would drive miles to gape at a native shrub or an animal that flourished only in a particularly disagreeable part of . . . [the] country." Information about the kling-kling bird inflamed his musical imagination. Before he left Jamaica he had his first song for the new show clearly in mind, "The Kling-Kling Bird on the Divi-Divi Tree."

By the time the ship was several days out of Jamaica, Moss Hart and Cole Porter had enough of a synopsis to be able to get to work in earnest. The time for sunbathing on deck chairs was over; even the time for talk. Now each became a prisoner in his own suite, trying to put his respective ideas down on paper.

"Almost immediately," said Hart, "a great change took place. Cole Porter, 'worker,' and Cole Porter, 'playboy,' were two different beings. . . . He worked around the clock. From the time I handed him the outline with the first two or three songs indicated, Cole seemed to withdraw . . . from the human race."

As the ship headed for the Fiji Islands, Cole Porter worked on "Begin the Beguine." "I had reservations about the length of the song," Hart said, after Porter had sung it through to him for the first time. "Indeed I am somewhat ashamed to record that I thought it had ended when he was only halfway through playing it."

Hart, as it turned out, was not the only one to underestimate "Begin the Beguine" on first hearing it.

By the time the cruise headed homeward the show was, to all intents and purposes, complete. Nevertheless, as invariably happens between the time a show is written and the time it comes to the stage, new situations, new dialogue, and new songs had to be added. One Saturday, while the show was being tried out in Ohio, Hart and Porter discussed the need for a new song in the second act. Hart hoped to have it within a week or two, but the following morning Porter brought him "Just One of Those Things." In spite of the speed with which it had been created, this song never had to be changed or altered. "It has been played and sung through the years," commented Moss Hart, "exactly as I heard it that Sunday afternoon in Ohio—a song written overnight."

The Moss Hart-Cole Porter musical comedy, *Jubilee*, opened at the Imperial Theatre in New York on October 12, 1935, with Mary Boland and Melville Cooper cast as the royal heads of a mythical kingdom. The show began to gain momentum at the box office and looked like a solid hit. Then Mary Boland was compelled to leave the cast to fill commitments in Hollywood. Since no replacement could be found for her, the show was forced to close after only 169 performances.

Strange to report, neither audiences nor critics took any note of its two best songs—which must always be numbered among the greatest Cole Porter ever wrote—"Just One of Those Things" and "Begin the Beguine." Both were introduced by June Knight, the latter as a duet with Charles Walter.

In fact, it appeared at first as if "Begin the Beguine" had been stillborn. It made no impression whatsoever during the run of the show and, after it closed, seemed to have been completely forgotten. Forgotten, that is, by everybody except a young jazz-band leader named Artie Shaw. In 1936 he signed a contract with RCA Victor to make records on the Bluebird label. As his first recording, the company wanted him to do a jazzed-up version of Rudolf Friml's "Indian Love Call." Shaw agreed—but only on the condition that on the "flip" side he be allowed to play Cole Porter's song, "Begin the Beguine." At first the recording director refused, maintaining that nobody knew "Begin the Beguine" and nobody was interested in it. But when Shaw stood his ground, the director relented, allowing himself to be convinced that the appeal of "Indian Love Call" in a strong beat might be able to carry the dead weight of "Begin the Beguine."

But in Artie Shaw's captivating presentation it was "Begin the Beguine" that started that record moving in the shops. Eventually it sold two million disks, the largest sale of any instrumental ever recorded by an American jazz group until then. "The recording of that one little tune," Artie Shaw has written, "was my real turning point." It was also the turning point for the Cole Porter classic, one of the dozen songs by which his greatness is always measured. In 1940, "Begin the Beguine" was interpolated into *The Broadway Melody*, the song-and-dance movie starring Fred Astaire and Eleanor Powell; in 1946 it was prominently featured in the Cole Porter screen biography *Night and Day*. When, in 1963, the American Society of Composers, Authors and Publishers (ASCAP) listed the sixteen songs which had proved the greatest money-makers in the half-century of that organization's existence, "Begin the Beguine" was one of two Cole Porter songs on that list, the other being "Night and Day." Porter himself said that of all the songs he had written his two favorites were "Begin the Beguine" and "Love for Sale."

DURING THE NINETEEN-THIRTIES, when Cole Porter was rapidly becoming one of the most successful as well as one of the most gifted composers and lyricists both on Broadway and in Hollywood, his pattern of life was organized to embrace work and play with equal fervor. In New York in the thirties, as in Paris in the twenties, he was a familiar figure at some of the season's leading social events; he was sought after for the most exclusive parties. "The small, lithe figure beautifully turned out, the intensely alive face, the immense dark eyes wonderfully set off by the . . . carnation in the lapel of his suit"—this was the way Moss Hart saw him. He added that Porter "had the gift of making any city singularly his own." The social elite, the upper crust of New York, swirled around him in the thirties as they had done in Paris a decade earlier.

A somewhat tired but elfin smile would be fixed on his lips. A sparkle would light up his brown saucerlike eyes. He would move among the great of the social, business, and artistic worlds with the grace and manner of one who had been born with a silver spoon in his mouth. When amused, his conversation was voluble, effervescent, and often brilliant. His speech was rapid and occasionally he lisped. At other times he wore an air of extreme boredom—boredom which Margaret Case Harriman once described as "spectacular." In the company of people who were scintillating or entertaining or profound, he gave of himself completely. But with people whose conversation dragged, studded with twice-told tales and ancient bromides, he would withdraw into himself until those around him felt he was in another room. Sometimes (without explanation or preliminary) he would even interrupt a speaker, put out his hand, and say a hurried good-by—leaving the startled individual in mid-sentence.

He smoked one cigarette after another. But his drinking was restricted to a dry Martini or an Amer Picon with lime juice before meals (Amer Picon being a favorite aperitif in Paris), or a glass or two of champagne at late-hour parties. His greatest social joy seemed to come from sparkling conversation and exquisite cuisine. Where food and drink were concerned he was a gourmet of gourmets. The food served in his home met the highest standards of the culinary art. Both Linda and Cole Porter went to fantastic lengths to get the recipe for any dish that tickled their palates. Once, while dining at Chasens' in Hollywood, Porter was impressed with the subtle taste of a chopped steak—a humble dish made poetic through the chef's imagination. The restaurant refused to give Porter the recipe, maintaining that it was a house secret. The next day, Porter's butler went to Chasens' and ordered chopped steak, which he wrapped carefully in a napkin and took home. Porter had it analyzed for its ingredients, then had his own chef prepare it for him.

His sartorial elegance, by day or night, was always pointed up by the carnation in his lapel. From the nineteen-twenties on that carnation was an inextricable part of his wardrobe. A touch of incongruity entered into his daytime dress, however, for then he always wore white socks, regardless of the color of the rest of his clothing. Those socks were Cole Porter's expression of respect to the memory of his grandfather, who had always worn white ones. Except for the carnation and the fashionable cut and tailoring of his clothes, Porter avoided swank or obvious display of wealth. He wore no jewelry. His only touch of ostentation was his gold cigarette case.

Though he was continually wandering to far-off

places—travel being a passion with which he never became satiated—Porter had not one home but three. One was his apartment on the forty-first floor of the Waldorf Towers, at the Waldorf Astoria Hotel on Park Avenue. This was one of several suites known as "Presidential" because they were reserved for the elect—for people like General Douglas MacArthur, ex-President Herbert Hoover, Ambassador Adlai Stevenson, and the Duke and Duchess of Windsor. Porter waited a full year to get his hands on one of those desirable apartments. When he did, he and Linda spent a quarter of a million dollars to decorate it to their satisfaction. The apartment, as might be imagined, was cluttered with *objets d'art* gathered the world over, together with a collection of great paintings, past and contemporary, both Porters being dedicated lovers of art. In fact, beautiful paintings were so basic to Cole Porter's happiness that whenever he was compelled to live in hotel suites out of town—usually during tryouts of his musicals—he took along several of his paintings with which to decorate his temporary living quarters. He even insisted upon bringing his own ash trays, since the commercial kind usually found in hotels repelled his esthetic tastes.

Since Porter functioned best in low temperatures, the Waldorf-Astoria apartment was always chilly—a condition Linda learned to tolerate in spite of the fact that she herself preferred a warmer temperature. Porter's partiality to coolness also led him to wear clothing of the lightest possible textures and fabrics. "I prefer going through life," he once said, "in paper clothes and icy rooms."

When the Porters were not setting off for foreign places, they made the Waldorf-Astoria apartment their home throughout the winter season, the focal point of their social activities, the base for Cole Porter's principal creative output. Every weekend, however, the Porters motored to their country cottage in Williamstown, Massachusetts. Then on June 11 each year—*always* June 11, though precisely why that day was chosen nobody knows—they moved on to their third house, a mansion in Brentwood, California, where they stayed until the fall. In these various places their personal needs were attended to by a valet, a butler, a maid, a chef, a household mistress, a chauffeur, and Cole Porter's secretary, Margaret Moore. The household was further enlarged by a schipperke named Pepe le Bref, a black dog which Merle Oberon, the motion-picture star, had presented to Porter; in time, Pepe le Bref had a companion, a second dog, Berthé.

The way in which year after year Porter went for his weekends to Massachusetts and to California on June 11 (that is, when he was not traveling abroad) points up the fact that he was a creature of habit. Once he started doing something, he kept on doing it methodically for years. When, for example, in the early nineteen-thirties, he started tuning in on a radio soap opera at four o'clock every day, he continued doing so for the rest of the decade, day after day, regardless of where or with whom he happened to be at the moment.

When reading, he wore tortoise-shell glasses; when writing, he worked left-handed on foolscap, surrounded by dictionaries, a thesaurus, and assorted writing equipment. Excessively tidy in all things, he insisted that everything on his desk be always in its proper place—from pencils to ash trays and the box of Kleenex. When working on a musical, he liked to keep the sheets of his music and lyrics neatly arranged in loose-leaf notebooks and Manila folders.

Work did not interfere with play—any more than play had interfered with work in the nineteen-twenties. He could attend three or four parties in a single night, but these social activities never delayed the process of completing any given assignment.

He had a terror of boredom, and was always fleeing from it. "I like hunting, swimming, parties, food, drink, cats, voyages," he once told an interviewer. "I like everything as long as it is different. And I *hate* boredom." Had he become bored, he insisted, he would have found it impossible to create.

He was a man of contagious enthusiasms whether for friends, a work of art, a new game, a new diversion, a prank, a new food, a performer, a choice night spot, a radio program, or somebody else's songs if they were good. Far from sapping his emotional responses, these enthusiasms gave him renewed vitality for the taxing demands of his creative chores. For of all his enthusiasms, the greatest one was for song writing.

The two worlds of Cole Porter—the social and the business—became one on opening nights of his musicals. Where other composers or playwrights became nervous, sometimes to the point of illness, Porter seemed to be the last word in relaxation. He commuted from backstage to the front, and again to the back, to supervise some final detail of production, to see that everything was in order, to greet and chat with his many friends and first-night guests. Then he sat through the performance with a calm and detachment which Russel Crouse once called "indecent"—almost as if he were watching somebody else's show. That detachment, however, was misleading. Behind that frozen and expressionless façade was a mind eagerly absorbing every phase of the production and noting those things, however trivial, that must be corrected or improved upon. After a lapse of years, Porter was able to remember every line of dialogue or lyric, every bit of show business, from any production.

Cole and Linda Porter avoided opening-night parties that are ritual on Broadway. They did not wait for the first newspaper notices that arrived on the street about 2 A.M. They preferred going home to their Waldorf-Astoria apartment, and having a quiet meal with champagne. They did not discuss the production, try to estimate the audience response or to guess the coming critical reaction. Linda's opinions always meant a good deal to Porter and they had discussed the show from every possible point of view while it was being written and rehearsed.

Early the next morning, they were awakened by Porter's valet who nodded approvingly if the newspaper reaction had been favorable, but shook his head sadly if not. Nothing more was said on the subject. The valet's gesture was always Porter's first indication of whether or not his show was going to be a hit.

IN THE MIDDLE NINETEEN-THIRTIES Porter's friends used to say of him: "Cole has wealth, genius, and a happy marriage. In fact, he has everything in the world except troubles."

Before the thirties were over Cole Porter had plenty of troubles, of a kind he was compelled to carry for the remainder of his life.

In 1937, while the Porters were guests at a house party given by the Countess Edith di Zoppola on her Long

Island estate, Porter and some friends went horseback riding. Porter was a skilled rider, but, while trying to negotiate a hill, his horse slipped in some mud and reared. He was thrown off. The horse fell on him.

"I was so stunned," Porter later recalled, "that I was unconscious of any great pain. In fact, strange as it may sound, while pinned under the horse and waiting for help, my mind was busily concocting some lines for a new lyric."

The accident proved serious. Both of Porter's legs were smashed. In addition, he had sustained a serious nerve injury. The pain was excrutiating, but not so bad as the omnipresent fear that both legs would have to be amputated. For a time he was plunged into such despair that he was almost suicidal. Despite the solicitude, tenderness, and encouragement that his wife—who never left his side—showered on him, he could not rid himself of the conviction that life was over for him.

In an effort to lift him out of his overwhelming melancholia and thoughts of self-destruction, the Broadway producers, the Shuberts, hurriedly contracted with him to write the score for a new musical comedy. They were convinced that Porter's only salvation was work and more work. They hoped that through creativity his will to live would be strengthened and he would be able to summon the courage necessary to triumph over his crippling disaster.

At first Porter refused to consider the idea. He insisted he was through—creatively as well as physically; he could not possibly summon from his broken and pain-wracked body the energy needed for writing a show. But Linda's urgings, arguments, and pleas proved stronger than Cole's doubts. He finally gave in. The piano in the Waldorf-Astoria apartment was raised on wood blocks to allow enough room underneath for his plaster casts, and so permit him to sit at the keyboard in the wheel chair, in which he was now a perpetual prisoner. Working called for Herculean effort on Porter's part, and an enormous expenditure of spirit and energy. He stuck to it—in spite of his physical agony.

When his songs had been written and the show went into rehearsal, many of the scenes had to be played in the apartment, since he was unable to go to the theater. From time to time the rehearsals had to stop abruptly because Porter was seized by a spasm of pain. The show opened at last at the Winter Garden on September 21, 1938. Called *You Never Know*, and having a cast headed by Clifton Webb and Lupe Velez, it was probably the worst musical comedy in which Cole Porter was ever involved; it had some of the worst songs he ever wrote; and it was his greatest box-office disaster.

"So you see," Porter told his wife sadly, "I am washed out completely. I have nothing left to give, and nothing left to do except to suffer."

Yet *You Never Know* was not a complete deficit. In fact, it had accomplished what the Shuberts had hoped it would. It had helped Porter rise above his physical handicaps and get back to a routine of work. It had stirred him once again to creativity and, in spite of his doubts, he frequently found himself concocting melodies and rhymes.

But his physical agony was not over by any means. To save his legs, Porter was compelled to undergo one serious operation after another. There were over thirty expeditions to the operating room within the next few years. For more than twenty months, he was bedridden in a hospital, his wife continually at his side. For five years after that he could move about only in a wheel chair, his legs having lost their mobility.

"Now I know fifty million Frenchmen can't be wrong," Porter remarked wryly to Linda after his first operation. "*They* eat horses—not ride them." But such excursions into levity were few and far between. Most of the time Porter was grim, with pain as his constant companion.

His physician, Dr. John J. Moorhead, convinced him of the necessity of not only plunging into work, even though under sedation most of the time, but also of resuming as far as possible his former social obligations and diversions. Linda did what she could to show her husband she was in full agreement with that. Both the physician and Linda encouraged Porter to return to the weekend routine of visiting his cottage in Massachusetts. But going to parties or taking short automobile trips, Porter and his wheel chair were inseparable.

The fact that, in spite of his almost continual suffering, he *was* able to resume his social life with little loss of personal charm and, in time, with a revived capacity for enjoying the good things of living, was miraculous enough. Perhaps more miraculous still was that he was able to get back to work at the highest level of his creativity. For while Porter was bedridden, alternating between sieges of physical torture and periods of mental dullness from pain-relieving drugs, he managed to complete one of his finest scores, for one of his most successful and brilliant musical comedies—*Leave It to Me*. This was a victory over pain and despair, and as Moss Hart said, it was in itself "a lesson in courage and gallantry" and a testament "to the greatness of the human spirit."

THE BOOK OF *Leave It to Me* was by Bella and Sam Spewack, their own adaptation of a stage comedy called *Clear All Wires*. The text was a spoof of the Soviet Union (the first time it was subjected to laughter in the American musical theater) and of the American diplomatic corps. Victor Moore was cast in the role of a blundering and excessively timid character who, through the maneuverings of an overambitious and domineering wife, was appointed America's Ambassador to the Soviet Union. He had no taste for the job. In fact, he was hopelessly homesick for Topeka, Kansas, and he spent most of his time yearning for such American delights as double banana splits. "Somebody in Washington mustn't like me," is his woebegone explanation for the plight in which he finds himself.

Determined to get back home, he concocts all kinds of international incidents and scandals to make his recall a virtual certainty. He insults the Nazi Ambassador and kicks him in the stomach; he shoots a Russian diplomat. Yet, to his horror, these events unexpectedly turn him into a national hero. The Russian diplomat he has shot, for example, turns out to be a Trotskyite spy—Trotskyites being the enemies of the existing regime bent on its destruction. Finally reconciled to his fate, he decides to give the ambassadorship his best efforts. In attempting to promote world peace and improve relations between the United States and the Soviet Union, he embarks on a series of statements, speeches, and actions which antagonize both countries and bring his diplomatic career to a sudden end.

The cast was studded with stars. Besides Victor Moore, there was William Gaxton to play the part of a brash American newspaperman; Tamara appeared as a vivacious French girl who has won the newspaperman's heart; and Sophie Tucker (now famous in night clubs as the "last of the red-hot mamas") was the Ambassador's overbearing wife. It was not one of these luminaries, however, who stole the show, but an unheralded young lady from Weatherford, Texas, making her Broadway debut in a minor role. She scored in a comparatively inconsequential scene contrived to allow stage hands to make a change of scene. The setting was a wayside railroad station in Siberia. Surrounded by five young men in fur jackets (one of them was Gene Kelly making the unpretentious New York stage debut that proved to be the first step toward stardom in Hollywood), this young lady, wearing ermine wraps, proceeded to do a mock strip tease as, in shrill, quivering baby tones, she sang "My Heart Belongs to Daddy". The show was stopped cold. The song became the hit number, the one to which, after opening night, audiences habitually looked forward with excited anticipation. And the formerly unknown singer soon became a blazing star in the theatrical firmament. Her name? Mary Martin.

She had made her stage debut singing "The Lilac Tree" in her native town in 1918, when she was only five. But her father, a successful lawyer, tried his best to keep out of her pretty little head any nonsense about going on the stage. He insisted that she get a thorough academic education, but she hated school from the beginning. At the Ward-Belmont School, which she attended in her late teens, she was interested only in dancing and singing.

Her formal education ended abruptly when she married her first husband, Benjamin Hagman, a boy from Fort Worth, Texas. And when that marriage ended five years later, as precipitously as her schooling had done, she conducted dancing classes in Weatherford. Finally she prevailed on her father to provide her with funds for a trip to Hollywood—her ambition, of course, to break into the movies. There she paid her bills by singing in small night clubs and in the Hotel Roosevelt Grill, and she appeared hopefully before so many Hollywood moguls that she came to be known as "Audition Mary." They all said she had neither the looks nor the personality to succeed in the movies.

One night, while performing at the Casanova night club in Hollywood, she was heard by Bing Crosby. He was so delighted with the way she sang "Shoe Shine Boy" that he had her repeat the chorus half a dozen times. Mary Martin was convinced that, through Crosby, the doors of the movie studios would swing wide open for her. But nothing happened.

Something *did* happen, however, when, in a Hollywood night spot, she gave a swing treatment to "*Les Filles de Cadiz*," a concert number favored by sopranos. The audience gave her a standing ovation, and the next day she received two offers. One of them was a contract for $250 a week to sing over the radio. The other was the more hazardous, since it guaranteed nothing—but it was the one she took: to come to New York and try out for a minor part in the new Cole Porter show, *Leave It to Me*. History and the critics recorded the rest.

Under a headline reading "Mary Martin a Find," Sidney Whipple wrote in the *World Telegram and Sun*: "Somewhere recently I read an advance suggestion that producers keep their eyes on a girl named Mary

Martin who has come on from Hollywood where, believe it or not, she did NOT appear in motion pictures. The suggestion was unnecessary. Anyone who can keep his eyes off her while she is singing her 'My Heart Belongs to Daddy' number is not a man and hence must be a mouse. She has the freshness and vitality of youth, but she also has poise and the gift of devilish humor, and I think she is a find."

The critic of the *Mirror* said: "Mary Martin enjoyed an individual triumph with her refreshing performance. . . . She is a welcome addition to the show sector with her bundle of tricks and numerous charms."

To have an unknown in a small part emerge as a star of stars was only one of the miracles of *Leave It to Me*, which became a Broadway hit of hits after opening on November 9, 1938. Those who knew Cole Porter intimately and who were fully aware of how he had worked on music and lyrics in spite of his terrible suffering, considered the high quality of his work a miracle in its own right. For Porter's contribution to the success of *Leave It to Me* was no minor one by any means.

"If Mr. Porter were not at the top of his form," said Brooks Atkinson in the New York *Times*, "the performers would probably have less of the grand manner. But he has written a score that is never routine for a moment—swift, smart and ingenious; and his lyrics sparkle."

Walter Winchell wrote in the *Mirror*: "It is Cole Porter's show from the moment the first asbestos lifts. He 'stopped' it several times with his Broadway ballads and other tuneful psalms. . . . Hit-proof words and music, to be sure."

In the New York *Herald Tribune*, Richard Watts, Jr. maintained: "Aided by one of Cole Porter's choicest scores . . . *Leave It to Me* proves to be a lively, tuneful and generally attractive musical comedy."

The last of the Cole Porter musical comedies in the nineteen-thirties—*Du Barry Was a Lady*—mocked French history. Bert Lahr appeared as a washroom attendant in a night club, secretly in love with its principal entertainer, played by Ethel Merman. Unable to win her in real life, he succumbs to dreams in which he is Louis XV and she is Madame du Barry. To the regal part of Louis XV, Bert Lahr brought all the rough-and-ready qualities that made him a comic *sui generis*: the amusing interjection of strange guttural sounds like "gang, gang, gang"; the colloquial speech; the grimaces and gestures as awkward as his diction.

He performed, said the critic Richard Watts, Jr., "with the sort of spluttering, indignant violence and leering impudence that makes him one of the best comedians in the world."

Ethel Merman contributed her own brand of lusty vigor to the part of Madame du Barry, and the combination of Lahr and Merman spelled a show that John Mason Brown called "a rowdy, boisterous, high-spirited extravaganza which stops at just this side of nothing and makes much of little."

Three of the Cole Porter songs had special interest.

One was a poignant ballad in a beguine rhythm, "Do I Love You?", which Ethel Merman sang with Ronald Graham. A second, also a duet—but this time for Ethel Merman and Bert Lahr—was "Friendship." The third was Ethel Merman's torrid show-stopping number, "Katie Went to Haiti."

In between his commissions for Broadway, Cole Porter began contributing scores for the Hollywood screen. As far back as 1929 he had written two original songs for a movie: "They All Fall in Love" and "Here Comes the Bandwagon" interpolated into *Battle for Paris* for Gertrude Lawrence. Between 1930 and 1936 Porter's only association with motion pictures came through screen adaptations of some of his successful Broadway musicals, including *Wake Up and Dream* and *Fifty Million Frenchmen* in 1931, *The Gay Divorcee* in 1934, and *Anything Goes* in 1936.

In 1936, Jack Cummings, a producer at M-G-M, signed Porter to write original songs for *Born to Dance*, a movie starring Eleanor Powell and James Stewart. This was the first time Cole Porter had been called upon by Hollywood to write a full score. Of the six numbers finally used, one was a standout—"I've Got You Under My Skin," sung by Virginia Bruce.

One year after that, Porter was contracted to write new songs for M-G-M's *Rosalie*, starring Eleanor Powell and Nelson Eddy. This was a movie adapted from a Broadway musical comedy which Florenz Ziegfeld had produced in 1928; in the stage show, the score had been shared by George Gershwin and Sigmund Romberg.

In making the transfer from stage to screen, M-G-M decided to use all new songs, and asked Cole Porter to come out to Hollywood to write them. From his score came two more hits, both introduced by Nelson Eddy: "In the Still of the Night" (a number distinguished by one of those characteristic exciting Cole Porter sweeps of melody midway in the chorus) and the title number, "Rosalie."

The paradox of the extraordinary success of that title number was that, in fashioning it, Cole Porter consciously imitated the clichés and stereotypes of his less-gifted competitors. He had written six different numbers called "Rosalie," each of which the producer of the movie had rejected as "too highbrow." Partly out of desperation, partly out of contempt, Porter decided to create something which pursued the stilted patterns adopted by so many song writers, both in the melody and the lyric. "Rosalie, my darling," the chorus began, "Rosalie, my dream." The melody was as humdrum as the words. To Porter's amazement not only did the producer consider the song ideal, but it became a fantastic success. Porter derived from this strange turn of events the same kind of mischievous pleasure that he once received from perpetrating a choice prank.

Before the decade was over, Porter—by that time an invalid—produced a second score for Jack Cummings for *The Broadway Melody of 1940*, its cast headed by Fred Astaire and Eleanor Powell. Released in 1939, this motion picture yielded a Cole Porter gem, "I Concentrate on You," sung by Douglas MacPhail.

Act Three
The Historic Forties

had reached their apex with the economic collapse of 1929. The "sober thirties" ended with the eruption of a World War in 1939.

On September 1 of that year, Nazi hordes invaded Poland by land and air. World War II—which had long menaced the thirties and which the world of diplomacy had vainly and at times desperately tried to avert—had finally exploded. The well-oiled German military machine moved relentlessly, crushing everything in its path. Warsaw fell after twenty-six days. Norway and Denmark were invaded the following April; the Netherlands, Belgium, and Luxembourg in May. When Paris fell on June 14, 1940, France was once again under the heel of German militarism. And England seemed to be lying helpless across the channel.

The free world was now neck-deep in a struggle for survival. In spite of the most devastating air attack the world had yet known, England not only remained standing erect, proud and free, but was soon able to summon the forces and the materials with which to retaliate. Then the Soviet Union was suddenly attacked by the Nazis, and the Japanese bombed the American bases at Pearl Harbor in Hawaii. The whole world was now in flames.

With more than ten million young Americans in uniform, with the nation's industry converted to war production, the global conflict dominated every possible phase of American life. People tightened their belts as rationing was instituted. A country that had learned to live on wheels stayed home to conserve gasoline and tires. Women left their kitchens and beauty parlors to work in war factories. War bonds were bought, air-raid drills were practiced, queues were formed for cigarettes and silk stockings. The people sang popular tunes in the spirit of these historic times, patriotic hymns like Irving Berlin's "God Bless America," martial songs like Frank Loesser's "Praise the Lord and Pass the Ammunition," and sultry ballads like Jule Styne's "I'll Walk Alone."

COLE PORTER WAS fighting a war of his own. In the early nineteen-forties he kept going in and out of hospitals for operations. He despaired completely of ever knowing a full day of relief from pain. But in his personal war he was proving a victor—for he was working on his songs harder than ever. In rapid succession, between 1940 and 1944, he wrote songs for four smash Broadway musicals; and at his best he produced pure Porter gold.

Those Cole Porter musicals reflected the way in which the war affected America. Of the four, three, in one way or another, had war plots.

The first was *Panama Hattie*, which started a run of over five hundred performances on October 23, 1940. Bud De Sylva, the successful song writer turned producer, had been impressed with the way Ethel Merman had sung "Katie Went to Haiti" in *Du Barry Was a Lady*. Convinced that a good musical comedy could be built around a character like Katie, with Ethel Merman playing the part, he took this suggestion to Porter. The composer was not sure such an idea was practical. He pointed out that a setting like Haiti could not provide a chorus line of attractive white girls and suggested a variation. Why not shift the scene to Panama? The more he thought of this change in locale, the more he liked it. Because of the Canal at Panama he felt a good story line might be built utilizing spy intrigues. De Sylva was delighted.

Herbert Fields was asked to work out a suitable libretto, in which Katie became Hattie, and Haiti became Panama. But as played by Ethel Merman, Katie was still the girl that went to Haiti. She wore, said Sidney Whipple in the New York *World Telegram and Sun*, "the same short, tight hobble skirt, with the same feather boa, and ostrich plumes and gaudy jewelry, and, at the beginning of the new show, with approximately the same set of morals."

The story of Panama Hattie concerned the efforts of foreign spies to blow up the Panama Canal. Their attempts, however, are finally thwarted by Hattie, a night-club singer who, by the time the final curtain descends, turns out to be as soft as velvet, with a heart of pure gold. Ethel Merman's performance—like the musical comedy which served as its frame—was full of brass fortissimo. As John Mason Brown said of her in the *New York Post*: "She dominates with all that strident precision which is hers and which is a happy example of our professional theater when it is functioning at its professional best."

But one of the most memorable moments in the show came not from the hard-boiled sequences or the characteristically vigorous Merman songs. It came rather from a poignant little number which Ethel Merman shared with an eight-year-old character played by little Joan Carroll. The song was called "Let's Be Buddies."

"There was a spot," Porter explained to an interviewer, in describing how this sequence came to be written, "where Joan Carroll and Ethel Merman had to sing and dance a duet. The spot required it. The law forbade it. The spot also stipulated that the song—as Ethel sang it—must be boozily sentimental in, of course, a ladylike way. So I wrote it that way, boozily sentimental to fit *Panama Hattie* and in a rhythm that could be walked to, in order to compensate for Joan having been prevented by law from dancing, and with a pattern in between so that Joan could recite instead of courting jail by singing. Also I put in an A-natural for Ethel because, while all her notes are extraordinarily good, A-natural is her best and the C above is a good finish for her."

Thus skillfully contrived to fit both the scene and its

players—and to meet the provisions of the child-labor law in New York—"Let's Be Buddies" turned out to be a "show-stopper."

"Gruff old codgers are going to choke a little this winter when tot and temptress sing 'Let's Be Buddies' and bring down the house," said Brooks Atkinson in his review.

"Let's Be Buddies" remained the high spot of the show when, in 1942, *Panama Hattie* was adapted for the screen (starring Ann Sheridan), and when, in 1954, it was made into a television spectacular over the CBS network, with Ethel Merman assuming her old role.

A significant footnote to American entertainment history was contributed by *Panama Hattie* one evening. Betty Hutton, who played a minor role and who had already won recognition as "public Jitterbug No. 1," was stricken with measles and could not perform. A young unknown by the name of June Allyson was picked out of the chorus line to take over her part. June performed with such aplomb, and so much personal charm, that she won the hearts of her audiences completely. "The greatest test came on the night when Betty, almost well again, sat in the box watching the show," Ethel Merman wrote some years later. "Most kids would have been scared silly, but not June. She played directly to Betty and performed like a trouper. I'd never seen an understudy take over with such confidence." After that, the young lady was neither a chorus girl nor an understudy any longer. One year after *Panama Hattie*, June Allyson became a Broadway star in *Best Foot Forward*, a musical produced by George Abbott. After that, her road led to Hollywood where she became a prime favorite in motion pictures and married Dick Powell.

Let's Face It in 1941 (547 performances) and *Something for the Boys* in 1943 (422 performances) both brought to the stage the American G.I. and his experiences in American military camps. The first of these musicals was set in Southampton, Long Island, near a fictional army installation, Camp Roosevelt. Three inductees get involved with three stately Long Island society matrons in an innocent flirtation—the matrons wanting to teach their wandering husbands a lesson.

When *Let's Face It* opened on October 29, 1941, America was not yet in the war. But the possibility of war preoccupied everybody, since national conscription or compulsory military service already had begun to pluck many an American out of civilian life and put him into an army camp. Frequent references to the vicissitudes, hardships, and personal upheavals in the life of an inductee gave *Let's Face It* both its topical interest and its humor. This was especially true with the character of Jerry Walker, played by Danny Kaye. Only a few months before *Let's Face It*, Kaye had become a Broadway star in *Lady in the Dark*. In *Let's Face It*, as a hapless inductee enmeshed in military routines and red tape, he once again demonstrated that he was a comedian with few rivals. As for songs by Cole Porter, two were particularly appealing: "Ace in the Hole" and "You

Irritate Me So", in each of which Nanette Fabray (already a star of musical comedy, but in later years to become one in television) participated zestfully.

By the time the first-night curtain rose on *Something for the Boys,* on January 7, 1943, America had been at war for over a year, and the American way of life had been radically transformed. Herbert Fields's text this time took in defense workers who had become a significant element in the war effort. Ethel Merman appeared as Blossom Hart, a night-club singer, who had taken a defense job. The plant she worked in was in Texas, only a stone's throw from an air base, Keeley Field. Inevitably, the paths of female defense workers and the Keeley military personnel crossed, of course with complications for all concerned. Blossom Hart fell into disrepute. Then she discovered that she was a human radio, thanks to the carborundum fillings in her dental bridgework. Thus she was able to save an airplane and its fliers from destruction. A heroine now, she captured the man of her heart, Sergeant Rocky Fulton, played by Bill Johnson.

In *Something for the Boys,* a comic rather than a romantic song was the Porter high light. It was called "By the Mississinewah." Here (for no apparent logical reason so far as explained by the plot) Ethel Merman and Paula Laurence appeared as squaws. With a generous interspersion of Indian "ughs" in their rendition, they sang about their husbands who were waiting for them back home in Indiana. Ethel Merman considers this one of the funniest songs she has ever presented, and Brooks Atkinson agreed with her in the New York *Times*.

The last of the quartet of the Cole Porter successes on Broadway in the early nineteen-forties was *Mexican Hayride* in 1944, with a run of 481 performances. This is the only one of the four productions which excluded suggestions of war. As its title indicates, the story is set in Mexico and involves a lady bullfighter (brilliantly enacted by June Havoc) with an American fugitive from justice (played with rollicking abandon by Bobby Clark), a shady speculator, and an American chargé d'affaires. The last of these, played by Wilbur Evans, provided the romantic interest with June Havoc. They introduced what became one of the leading love ballads of 1944, "I Love You". Two other Cole Porter numbers, "Sing to the Guitar" and "Carlotta", had greater atmospheric than musical interest. Consequently, though they played an important part in the production, and embellished it, they are two of Porter's least familiar songs.

Cole Porter's greatest song hit during the war years—indeed, one of the greatest commercial successes of his entire career—did not come out of a Broadway show. It was a curiosity. For one thing, both in melody and in lyrics, it was not in the usual Cole Porter suave manner; for another, it was not distinguished by Porter's partiality for the unexpected turn of phrase and line. In fact, Porter wrote it with tongue square in cheek—primarily for his own amusement.

One day, in the nineteen-thirties, he was listening to some radio music. A popular song in the style of a cowboy ballad by turns amused and irritated him with its mawkish sentimentality and its profusion of cowboy clichés. Then and there he decided to satirize this kind of number, so he wrote "Don't Fence Me In."

The song was supposed to be used in a motion picture, *Adios Argentina*, but the picture was never released and Porter forgot all about the song. Almost a decade later, however, it was sung as a serious cowboy ballad (*not* as a parody) by Roy Rogers in *Hollywood Canteen*, a motion picture released in 1944. Then things started to happen. Kate Smith sang it over the air and was swamped with letters and phone calls of congratulations. Bing Crosby and the Andrews Sisters made a recording for Decca that sold over a million disks in 1944. Frank Sinatra also made a highly successful recording. By 1945, the song had become so popular that Republic Pictures built a movie around it, starring Roy Rogers and called it *Don't Fence Me In*. Meanwhile, on radio's Hit Parade, "Don't Fence Me In" held the top spot for several weeks running.

ALTHOUGH FROM TIME to time Cole Porter wrote songs because a subject, incident, remark, or turn of phrase caught his fancy, he derived his strongest creative stimulation from a musical-comedy text or a motion-picture scenario; a character, situation, or piece of stage business often inspired the songs to be used within a given production. One might be written to allow time to change a scene, as was "My Heart Belongs to Daddy" in *Leave It to Me*. "I Love

Paris", written for *Can-Can* in the nineteen-fifties, drew its inspiration from a stage set.

Some songs were tailor-made to suit a specific voice. In "I Get a Kick Out of You", for instance, the repeated use of the notes A-flat, B-flat and C natural took advantage of Ethel Merman's best tones. The limited vocal range of "Night and Day" conforms to Fred Astaire's singing style. Some songs were intended to bring out a certain facet of a character's personality; some, to strengthen the motivation of the plot; some to heighten the mood or intensify the atmosphere of a given scene.

But despite the immediate purpose of a given Cole Porter song within a musical comedy or motion picture —despite the fact that a few were written with lightning speed—the truth is that many of Porter's songs, and some of his best ones, were rooted in his past experiences in foreign lands and with interesting people. His mind was an inexhaustible storehouse from which, at any given moment, he seemed able to pluck out an episode, a piece of conversation, a phrase casually overheard, a setting, even a sound. Ideas for songs lay dormant with Porter, sometimes for years, to emerge full grown in the proper setting or conditions.

Do you remember the mythical characters, Mr. and Mrs. Fitch, that Cole Porter created to mock the Parisian social set? Well, some years later, Mr. and Mrs. Fitch were reincarnated in a song for *The Gay Divorce*. It was called "Mr. and Missus Fitch" and was intended to spoof social climbers. Another prank was the source of one other song. One evening, in 1934, while attending a party in New York, Cole Porter was amused by the way in which his bearded friend, Monty Woolley, tried to pass himself off as a butler. Porter went over to the piano and then and there improvised the words and music of "Miss Otis Regrets"—the staid and formal announcement by a butler that Miss Otis was unable to lunch today because she has just shot her lover, and had to be dragged off to jail. Woolley proceeded at once to learn words and music, and delivered them for the delighted company that same evening with mock pomposity. For the rest of the season Woolley enjoyed coming to parties dressed up as a butler and chanting "Miss Otis Regrets" as he entered. Porter never used this sardonic number in any of his shows, but it was interpolated for Monty Woolley in the Cole Porter screen biography *Night and Day*.

Remembered phrases or remarks frequently served as a reservoir from which Porter drew song ideas. Once, in Monte Carlo, he was amused by the way the glamorous actress, Peggy Joyce Hopkins, repeated the phrase "for instance who?" Some years later, that phrase cropped up in his song "It Ain't Etiquette", originally intended for *Du Barry Was a Lady* (though it did not finally appear there). *It's De-lovely* and *Well, Did You Evah!* are two other phrases which became the titles of songs—one for *Red, Hot and Blue* and the other for *Du Barry Was a Lady*—long after Porter had overheard people using them and had committed them to memory.

Once a wager was responsible for the birth of a song. In any event that was how Porter happened to write

"I Love You" for *Mexican Hayride.* He desperately needed a love ballad for the show, but, in spite of many attempts, he had failed to come up with something that he felt would serve. The producer of *Mexican Hayride* was Michael Todd—the same man who, just before his death in 1958 in an airplane disaster, made motion-picture history with *Around the World in Eighty Days.* Todd asked Porter which title was the most frequent cliché in songs, to which the composer replied without hesitation: "I love you."

Todd exclaimed, "Cole, I'm willing to make a bet with you that you can take such a cliché title, use only three notes, one for each word, improvise a two-finger exercise as accompaniment—and come up with a smash song hit."

Porter smiled skeptically.

"Well," continued Todd, "I'm still willing to put money on the line that you can do it."

Porter took the bet—and lost. He did manage to write a major hit—in fact probably the leading song hit of 1944—with "I Love You" as the title, as the principal phrase in the chorus, and with only three notes for that phrase.

Porter's around-the-world wanderings probably were the most fruitful source of all for song materials. Since he was fond of far-off, glamorous places, many of his song classics have an exotic character. "What Is This Thing Called Love?" was based on a chant Porter had heard in Marrakech, Morocco; and we know that the rhythms of distant Moroccan drumbeats gave him the idea for "Night and Day." "Begin the Beguine" owed its origin to some native music he came across on the island of Kalabhi in the Dutch East Indies. "Katie Went to Haiti" was derived from sounds produced by a native band in Haiti. Snatches of melodies picked up in Bali contributed to a ballet sequence in *Jubilee*. And, as noted earlier, Porter's investigations of the kling-kling bird in Jamaica made it possible for him to write "The Kling-Kling Bird on the Divi-Divi Tree."

One evening while supping with friends at *Le Boeuf sur le toit* in Paris, Porter amused himself by joining Mrs. Alistair Mackintosh in improvising in rhyme all kinds of superlatives in various fields of endeavor. When one of the scenes in *Anything Goes* required the night-club entertainer and the playboy to exchange saucy compliments, Porter suddenly recalled the little game he had played with Mrs. Mackintosh—and so he was able to produce "You're the Top."

Cole Porter often told interviewers that his greatest inspiration came from a signed contract. Once he knew he had to write with a purpose, his mind began to burst with ideas like exploding fireworks. His alert, creative brain kept working all the time: while he shaved, while he was riding in a taxi, even at parties. He worked out the general design, and sometimes even the details, of each of his songs in his head before going to a piano or using pencil and paper. For this reason it was possible for him to work while appearing to entertain friends at home or being a guest at a party. Sometimes when he was engaged in a polite conversation, an intriguing idea for a song suggested itself. He would suddenly withdraw into himself without warning—"out of sight, out of the room, out of the city" is the way one of his friends described it—and begin then and there to work out the material to its fullest potential. His eyes became glazed and his eyelids drooped; his face became blank, a mechanical smile frozen on it; he would seem at the moment to be the most bored man in the world. But what he was actually doing was—working.

While dreaming up his songs, whether the lyrics or the melody, his powers of concentration were so intense that he was aware of nothing but the creative problem absorbing him at the moment. Once, during the rehearsal of a musical, his collaborator, Russel Crouse, became convinced that he had seriously offended Porter. Crouse had passed by him a dozen times but never once, by any sign or gesture, had Porter given any indication of having recognized him. The thirteenth time, however, Porter suddenly emerged from his trance to greet Crouse brightly and warmly. "I've just worked out a brand-new lyric, Russel," he announced.

In an interview, Porter once described his *modus operandi* as follows: "First I think of an idea for a song and then I fit it to a title. Then I go to work on a melody, spotting the title at certain moments in the melody. Then I write the lyric—the end first—that way it has a strong finish. It's terribly important for a song to have a strong finish. I do the lyrics the way I'd do a crossword puzzle. I try to give myself a meter which will make the lyric as easy as possible to write, but without being banal. . . . I try to pick for my rhyme words of which there is a long list with the same ending."

Sometimes a complete song became fixed in mind in half an hour; sometimes it took days. Only when it was all of one piece did Porter try to play it through on the piano. At the same time, he sang the lyrics in a metallic and (his own description) "unpleasant" voice. When he liked a song, he performed with considerable gusto. When he was not sure of it, his rendition was nervous, tense, and halting.

He always demonstrated an extraordinary capacity for hard and sustained work. He required only a few hours' sleep, usually between sunrise and ten in the morning. Between eleven and five during the day his time and energies were given to creative labors. Ideas were finalized on paper. Hours were spent in detailed and extended revisions if these were necessary, and much of this editing was done while Porter lay on a couch staring blankly at the ceiling.

IF THE FIRST HALF of the forties had brought Cole Porter nothing but success, the latter half—at least up to 1948—was marked only by failure. Between December, 1944, and December, 1948 Porter had two shows on Broadway: *The Seven Lively Arts* produced by Billy Rose in 1944 with a stellar cast headed by Beatrice Lillie and Bert Lahr; *Around the World*, in 1946, with text by Orson Welles.

There was little to commend in either of them and both collapsed at the box office.

Out in Hollywood, Porter hardly did any better. The only picture for which he contributed a complete score was *The Pirate*, released in 1948. It proved a bore, even though starring Judy Garland and Gene Kelly and though one song from it—"Be a Clown"—had a mild success. To compound disaster no other song from any of these productions had won public favor, for the very sound reason that none was worthy of Cole Porter.

Both on Broadway and in Hollywood one's success is measured by one's most recent production. By 1948 the "wise men" of show business were beginning to whisper that Cole Porter was through. They summoned many varied and impressive reasons as to why this was so. The seemingly endless round of operations on his legs, and the seemingly perpetual bout with pain, they said, had finally sapped Porter's creative strength; the only thing to wonder at, they continued, was that this had taken so long to happen.

Broadway's cognoscenti also pointed out that the kind of musical comedy for which he had long been satisfied to write his songs had become outmoded. This was musical comedy where the text counted for little and was manufactured just to provide an excuse for good songs, comedy routines, and dances; to offer outstanding stars ample opportunities to strut their stuff. The characters, background, and atmosphere were as synthetic as the plot. Cole Porter musicals sought to provide entertainment, not to aim for originality, credibility, or artistic levels. If a piece of stage business, a piece of music, a dance or a comedy sequence had audience appeal, it was used, even if it had no relevancy within the story. A good case in point was the Indian number "By the Mississinewah," included in the musical comedy about defense works and army air pilots, which we have already discussed.

If any of Cole Porter's musical comedies had distinction, it was mainly because he happened to be one of the most gifted, original, and inventive composers and lyricists. Thus he could contribute to most of his productions songs of the highest caliber, though by themselves, the musical comedies had nothing new to say. Porter was satisfied with such a state of things. In working for the stage, he was far more concerned about bringing his personal approach and brilliance of thought to a bit of verse or to the development of a melodic line than he was with the artistic quality of the texts or situations for which his songs were intended.

But—so contended many of Broadway's lights in contemplating Cole Porter's alleged decline and fall—the musical theater had not stood still, even if Porter had. Shows like *Show Boat*, the beautiful musical play by Oscar Hammerstein II and Jerome Kern, in 1927; incomparable political satires like *Of Thee I Sing*, in 1931, songs by George and Ira Gershwin, text by George S. Kaufman and Morrie Ryskind—the first musical comedy to win the Pulitzer Prize; in 1943, the Rodgers and Hammerstein masterwork, *Oklahoma!*, a folk play with music that uncovered new vistas for the musical theater—all these represented for the stage something brave and new to which audiences were responding with far greater excitement and enthusiasm than they had shown for the older, formalized kind of musical comedy.

In this new genre of the musical theater, the whole was more important than any of its parts. The play—the situations, the background, the characters—determined what kind of material should be used, and not vice-versa. The only music, dance, comedy, and production numbers tolerated were those which were basic to the plot, which helped to carry the story line, and which served to project the mood or intensify the emotion. "Integration" was a word now being bandied about to point up a musical which was all of a single design. No longer could songs, stars, sets, or costumes by themselves carry the dead weight of a plot that depended for its denouement on all kinds of unbelievable coincidences and accidents, and of characters that seemed to be built from the same kind of cardboard and papier mâché as comprised some of the sets.

They were saying along Broadway in the middle nineteen-forties that Cole Porter, as composer and lyricist, was just too much of an individualist to allow his songs to play a secondary role to text and characters; he was not the kind of creator who would delete a number to which he was particularly partial just because it had no logical place in the over-all context. In the new scheme of things along Broadway, they said,

Cole Porter had a place no longer, because no longer could a song like "Night and Day" carry a whole production singlehandedly. Now the play, and not the song, was *the* thing.

The cynics and the skeptics on Broadway had still another valid reason for thinking that Cole Porter's day had ended. He had been a voice of the "roaring twenties" which somehow had managed to carry the rakish spirit of that epoch into the "sober thirties." His greatest songs, during the thirties, reverberated with the infectious, abandoned, and devil-may-care attitudes that the twenties had glorified; they continued to approach life (now grown so much more serious) with the impudent laughter of the twenties. But as that decade receded into the forgotten past, brushed aside by the sterner problems of the thirties and then the early forties, the Cole Porter song—however brilliant—was proving an anachronism.

The cynics said that the Cole Porter way with a lyric and a melody could never cope with the grim realities of a depression and a war. They pointed to the fact that, though he had provided the scores for three musical comedies about the impact of the war on the American way of life in the early nineteen-forties, not one of the songs in any of these productions had been in tune with these stirring martial times; all of them were just echoes of a departed era. The times had moved quickly, they said, but Cole Porter still lived and wrote as if the twenties had never ended.

That Porter's day *had* been magnificent, the skeptics

did not doubt. This fact had been emphasized—if, indeed, it needed any emphasizing—by the motion picture produced by Warner Brothers and released in 1946. *Night and Day* was intended as a screen biography of the composer, starring Cary Grant as Porter. The story was one of those concoctions created synthetically to provide an excuse for the presentation of Cole Porter's hit parade. The basic biographical facts were there—from Yale to the Foreign Legion, from the carefree days in Paris to the tragic accident on Long Island; and Cary Grant's characterization did manage to capture some of Porter's *joie de vivre* and urbanity.

"With Cary Grant giving a casual and thoroughly ingratiating performance as the gifted song writer," said the New York *Times*, "the new technicolor opus . . . moves with slick cinematic and rhythmical ease from one Porter hit-tune show to another. . . . While *Night and Day* begs quick dismissal as an idealistic smattering of biography about a living person, there is no denying it is stuffed with the gaudy things that make for a visually handsome entertainment . . . rather thin and conventional . . . concocted about the fabulous Mr. Porter."

It was the songs—fourteen of them—that proved the glory of the production and gave it its greatest significance and fascination. Here audiences and critics were confronted with a cross section of Porter's creative genius through the years, beginning with the early "Old-Fashioned Garden," including such little-known curiosities as "Miss Otis Regrets" (which Monty Woolley presented in much the same way as he used to do at parties in the thirties); recalling how Mary Martin had brought down the house with "My Heart Belongs to Daddy"; and covering such classics as "Begin the Beguine," "What Is This Thing Called Love?," "Just One of Those Things," "In the Still of the Night," "You're the Top" and "I've Got You Under My Skin." It was this magnificent procession of song that led Howard Barnes of the *Herald Tribune* to say, "*Night and Day* is definitely on the beam."

But, said Porter's critics, such magnificence and greatness was a thing of the past; the future offered a challenge a man like Cole Porter could not meet. Porter himself recognized that challenge posed by the changing times and theater. "The librettos are much better," he told an interviewer after *Oklahoma!* had opened so triumphantly, "and the scores are much closer to the librettos than they used to be. Those two—Rodgers and Hammerstein—have made it much harder for everybody else."

But Cole Porter had proved himself victorious over physical pain and years of life as an invalid. He was certain he could triumph over the artistic challenges as well. So he proceeded to silence his critics once and for all by creating the greatest musical score of his career in what proved to be one of the most successful musical stage productions in Broadway history—*Kiss Me, Kate.*

AT THE BEGINNING, as it was being crystallized, *Kiss Me, Kate* did not promise much. The producers—Saint Subber and Lemuel Ayers—were novices at the game of putting on shows; and to make matters worse, they had few financial resources of their own, and no backing. Ordinarily, a composer of Cole Porter's stature would not think of starting negotiations with such neophytes. But Porter, tragic to say, was not in a chooser's position any longer.

It seemed that the successful producers had forgotten that Cole Porter had written the songs for a long skein of successes since *Fifty Million Frenchmen,* almost twenty years earlier; they had forgotten that only a few years ago Cole Porter had enjoyed four smash musical-comedy successes in a row. With characteristic Broadway capacity to take into consideration only the immediate present, all that could now be remembered was that the last two productions with Porter music had been failures and that he had not come up with a Hit Parade song for some time. For these reasons Porter had become something of an untouchable. He had waited for offers that had not come—until Saint Subber and Lemuel Ayers approached him with *Kiss Me, Kate.* After talking the matter over with his wife at great length, Porter came to the conclusion—not without some despair—that he had to seize this opportunity, even though it was offered by novices in the theater. As his wife told him firmly, "After all, Cole, it isn't the producer who *makes* a Cole Porter show. It's Cole Porter."

The project itself did not at first glance look particularly inviting. *Kiss Me, Kate* was to be a musical-comedy adaptation of the Shakespeare play, *The Taming of the Shrew,* a concoction devised by Bella and Sam Spewack. Shakespeare into musical comedy? Well, it had been done once before, and quite successfully and brilliantly at that—when Rodgers and Hart, in 1938, had written and produced *The Boys from Syracuse* based on *The Comedy of Errors.* But translating Shakespeare into modern musical-comedy terms was such a ticklish proposition that nobody since then had tried to do it again.

To complicate matters still further for the new show —at least where Porter was concerned—*Kiss Me, Kate* was conceived by its librettists along the lines of the "new" musical theater, in the style of *Oklahoma!* Bella and Sam Spewack did not just rewrite *The Taming of the Shrew* and update it with songs and dances. They worked out a highly original and intriguing plan. Parts of Shakespeare's sixteenth-century play—with costumes and scenery from old Padua in Italy—alternated with scenes of contemporary American interest and with contemporary American characters. All this was achieved by having an American theatrical company of our own day present the Shakespeare comedy in Baltimore, the action shifting back and forth from an actual performance of the Shakespeare play to the backstage goings on of a modern theatrical troupe.

Such a text was far different from any with which Cole Porter had ever been involved. The other musical-comedy books had been shallow, superficial, and synthetic—a dummy decked out in finery. The Spewack text was a "book show"—that is, an "integrated" production in which every element of the musical theater was subservient to plot and characters. Would Porter be able to curb his virtuoso instincts as composer and lyricist and play second fiddle to the librettists? Many of those who heard about the kind of show *Kiss Me, Kate* was insisted that it just was not Cole Porter's nature to suppress a flashing set of brilliant rhymes or a sure-fire Porter melody (assuming, of course, he was still capable of these, which a good many of his critics doubted) just because there might not be a logical place for them in the play.

If there were doubts about the capabilities of young and inexperienced producers to mount a successful show, or about the willingness of Cole Porter to submit to the requirements of the new integrated kind of musical comedy, there were even greater ones inspired by the casting. Alfred Drake (who had risen to stardom in *Oklahoma!*) had the leading male role. He was, however, coming to the new musical after having suffered a series of failures on Broadway. Certainly he was no longer a drawing card. And Patricia Morison, chosen for the role of the heroine, had never before been starred in a Broadway production. Her only other earlier Broadway appearance had been in 1938 in an operetta that had been a box-office fiasco. Lisa Kirk and Harold Lang, selected for subsidiary roles, had proved themselves respectable performers—Lisa Kirk in the Rodgers and Hammerstein musical play *Allegro;* Harold Lang in several minor musical-comedy productions. But not even their strongest admirers would say that either one was the kind of magnet that could draw customers into a theater.

The unhappy combination of inexperienced producers, a composer and a leading man who were on the decline, a leading lady who was not known to most theatergoers—all this added up to a commodity which would be difficult, if not impossible, to sell to potential backers. It took more than a year, and twenty auditions, to find some seventy investors ready to pool the sum of $180,000 needed for the production.

Then there took place one of those miracles that make Broadway the exciting and unpredictable place it is. Once rehearsals began, things fell magically into place. Alfred Drake, Patricia Morison, Lisa Kirk, Harold Lang suited one another as neatly and perfectly as parts of a jigsaw puzzle put into their proper places. John C. Wilson's astute direction sparked them into giving the performance of their lives. He kept the action moving fluidly from the past to the present, from Padua to Baltimore. Hanya Holm contrived some of the most exciting dances the Broadway stage had witnessed since *Oklahoma!* Lemuel Ayers provided scenic and costume designs that were breath-takingly beautiful and colorful. Dialogue and song blended as naturally as did the past and present into an inextricable musico-dramatic entity. *Kiss Me, Kate* was supreme "integration"—a musical play in every sense of that term as opposed to old-fashioned musical comedy.

The curtain rises on a theatrical troupe come to Baltimore, Maryland, to present Shakespeare's *The Taming of the Shrew*. The leading performers of this company are Fred Graham (played by Drake) and his former wife, Lilli (Patricia Morison); Bill Calhoun, a chronic gambler (Harold Lang), and his girl friend, Lois Lane (Lisa Kirk). Bill confesses to Lois that he has lost $10,000 in a crap game and has given some gangsters an I.O.U. which he cannot possibly redeem. He is convinced that the gangsters will give him short shrift. Lois is upset, particularly since this is not the first time Bill has been in trouble through gambling. "Why Can't You Behave?" she sings to him softly.

Fred Graham and his ex-wife have problems. Though divorced, they are still emotionally involved with each other. Nostalgically they recall, in the song "Wunderbar," how they had once performed together in Vienna. With the opening night of *The Taming of the Shrew* imminent, Fred sends a bouquet of flowers to his star, Lois Lane. By mistake the flowers land in Lilli's dressing room. This convinced Lilli that Fred is still in love with her. Her own tenderness for Fred is revealed in the ballad "So in Love."

Then the scene shifts to the actual performance of *The Taming of the Shrew*. After the ensemble is heard in the number, "We Open in Venice," the Shakespearian plot begins to unfold. In old Padua, the two sisters, Bianca and Katharina, want to get married, but Bianca must wait her turn until her older sister has found a husband. They contemplate possible candidates in "Tom, Dick and Harry." Petruchio, meanwhile, arrives in Padua in search of a wealthy mate, as he lightly explains in "I've Come to Wive it Wealthily in Padua." When Petruchio is finally chosen for Katharina, she makes it perfectly clear, in "I Hate Men," how repulsive she finds all males. Petruchio, for his part, in "Were Thine That Special Face," discloses that Katharina is not to his liking. Despite this mutual lack of interest, the match is arranged for them.

At this point, the action in the musical play shifts back to present-day Baltimore, and to the complications that entangle the personal lives of the performers. Lilli has discovered that Fred's flowers were intended for Lois. In a furious temper, she swears she is leaving the theatrical company for good.

At the rise of the second-act curtain we are carried back into the Shakespeare comedy as performed by the theatrical troupe. Now man and wife, Petruchio and Katharina are continually embroiled in hot quarrels, since Katharina has turned out to be an incorrigible shrew. Longingly—in "Where Is the Life That Late I Led?"—Petruchio looks back to those happy days when he was single. A return to twentieth-century Baltimore finds Bill and Lois also quarreling, but for different reasons. He accuses her of flirting with other men in the cast. In "Always True in My Fashion" she makes light of her fickle nature. The precipitous acceptance of the gangsters backstage plunges Bill into despair. Miraculously, however, things take a turn for the better with the news that a shake-up in the gangster world has reduced his I.O.U. to mere scrap paper. Bill and Lois, delighted at this turn of affairs, fall in each other's arms. Back again in the Shakespeare play, Petruchio tames Kate by outmatching her in tempers, moods, whims, and caprices, while in today's Baltimore Fred and Lilli realize that they can no longer live apart.

Though it had taken Cole Porter only three months to write all the songs for *Kiss Me, Kate,* his score, as Walter Kerr described it in the *Herald Tribune,* was "one of the loveliest and most lyrical yet composed for the contemporary stage." Both as a composer and as a lyricist Porter was at the height of his creative powers. Never before had he produced for a single show so many song hits—and in so many different styles.

In some of his songs for *Kiss Me, Kate,* Porter wrote in the vibrant present. In others, placed within the performance of *The Taming of the Shrew,* he neatly caught the flavor of old Padua—by lifting a line, perhaps taking over a random thought, expropriating just a suggestion from Shakespeare. In such a category we find "Where Is the Life That Late I Led?" and "I've Come to Wive it Wealthily in Padua" and "Were Thine That Special Face." In some of his songs he was romantic, in some satiric, in some witty, in some urbane, and in some atmospheric.

"Veins tapped successfully in earlier shows," as I said in *Panorama of American Popular Music,* "stood out more prominently than ever. Rarely were his moods more darkly indigo than in 'So in Love'; rarely had his flair for parody and satire been so prominent as in 'Wunderbar' (a charming take-off on the Viennese waltz), and in 'Always True to You in My Fashion'; rarely did he leap with such agility and gaiety to broad humor and burlesque as in 'Brush Up Your Shakespeare' and 'I Hate Men'; rarely before did he manage to be as torrid and combustible as in 'Too Darn Hot.' "

In fact, there was hardly a song style that could not be found among the seventeen numbers comprising the score. More remarkable still, there was hardly one number that was not top-drawer Porter. This score was his masterwork. Never again was he to match this Olympian achievement.

There were two good reasons why Porter was finally able to rise above the slough of mediocrity into which he had been pulled for a number of years. The exciting novelty and the consistent brilliance of the Spewack text—one of the best in the history of the American musical theater—was the spark Porter needed to set his own creative imagination aflame. He had never before had such stimulation. Whatever barriers may have hemmed in his creativity were broken down to allow the flood of his musical and poetical ideas to overflow.

In addition to this, the year of 1948 provided the kind of climate in which Porter could flourish. What his severest critics had said about him just before *Kiss Me, Kate* was perfectly true: Porter's sophisticated songs were never well suited for laments about the Depression or stirring hymns about the war. He sang best in and about times like the twenties when life was to be enjoyed to the full. The era that followed World War II (as we pointed out in the opening of this book) was also such an era. The release from war tensions, the expanding economy, the frenetic pursuit of pleasure and luxurious living—all this and more generated the same kind of heady spirit that had once characterized the twenties. This was a spirit that Cole Porter could catch and fix in melody and lyrics as nobody else in the world could.

THE CRITICS HEAPED accolades on *Kiss Me, Kate* and on Cole Porter. Howard Barnes said in the *Herald Tribune*: "There is next to nothing wanting in *Kiss Me, Kate,* the proud and exultant musical comedy which has opened at the Century Theater."

William Hawkins of the *World Telegram* said: "*Kiss Me, Kate* is gay, beautiful, tuneful and plenty more. . . . Cole Porter has turned out one of his all-time best scores."

Variety reported: "The smash success of *Kiss Me, Kate* (and it is unquestionably a smash) is a thrilling story of show business—the triumphant return of Cole Porter, the prodigal composer, to the ranks of theatrical greats. . . . Porter has made his comeback with the finest score of his career."

Brooks Atkinson agreed in the New York *Times* that this was Cole Porter's best score, and his wittiest lyrics, adding: "The Italian setting . . . gives Mr. Porter an opportunity to poke beyond Tin Pan Alley into a romantic mood. Without losing his sense of humor he has written a remarkably melodious score with an occasional suggestion of Puccini, who was a good composer, too. Mr. Porter has always enjoyed the luxury of rowdy tunes and he has scribbled a few for the current festival . . . fresh out of the honky tonks. All his lyrics are literate. . . . But the interesting thing about the new score is the enthusiasm Mr. Porter has for the romantic melodies indigenous to the soft climate of the Mediterranean."

With such a rhapsodic send-off, *Kiss Me, Kate,* which opened on December 30, 1948, became one of the most successful musicals in stage history. It entered the golden circle of thousand-performance shows (1,077 performances to be exact). The original-cast recording for Columbia sold over a million long-playing disks. In 1952, the show became a lavish, colorful, briskly paced motion picture, produced by M-G-M, starring Kathryn Grayson and Howard Keel. Bosley Crowther described it in the New York *Times* as "one of the year's most magnificent films . . . a beautifully staged, adroitly acted, and superbly sung affair." In 1956, *Kiss Me, Kate* was successfully revived in New York, to be greeted anew by hosannas, as if it were being seen for the first time.

Kiss Me, Kate made the rounds of European musical capitals in foreign translations; in many of these places it was the first American musical comedy to be produced. Late in 1955 it was seen at the renowned Staatsoper in Berlin (home of grand opera) where it took the audience by storm. It then became the first all-German showing of an American musical comedy ever to be given in Berlin—and after that in other German cities as well. On February 14, 1956 (in still another German translation), it was mounted handsomely at the Volksoper in Vienna.

"The enthusiastic first-night audience applauded, stamped and cheered," reported the New York *Times* from a cable. "One critic . . . predicted that the American musical would conquer the European operetta stage as jazz had done the dance floor."

Its sixty-one performances comprised the longest run enjoyed by any musical production in the history of Vienna state theaters; and its take at the box office was the largest of any show seen at the Volksoper during its sixty years of existence. Julius Rudel, who conducted the Viennese production, became convinced that *Kiss Me, Kate* would have "effects on the writing and staging of future productions in Vienna. It served to acquaint the Viennese with the use of music of many different forms in a single show, with the careful integration of music and book, with the sustaining of a constant performance without long pauses, and with the use of a singing chorus that is moving all the time, always participating, never standing around. These were the basic revolutions in 'operetta' production that Vienna witnessed and loved, and which doubtless will affect the future of its musical stage."

After that, *Kiss Me, Kate* became the first American musical comedy ever produced in Poland. In Scandinavia, it started a run which, on and off, was to continue for about ten years. Opening in Budapest, late in 1963, it became the biggest theatrical hit that city had known in several seasons. In the summer of 1963, *Kiss Me, Kate* went to Turkey, playing to packed houses in Ankara, Istanbul, and Izmir. "Lines a block long wind towards the box-office whenever a performance of *Kate* is coming up," reported Jay Walz to the New York *Times* from Turkey. "Lines are still there when the last tickets have been sold." It was Walz's belief that the show would run for a number of years if it were to satisfy all the customers who wanted to see it.

By 1964, *Kiss Me, Kate* was being heard abroad in its eighteenth foreign language. And still the march around the world was to continue—for later in 1964 performances in native languages were being scheduled for Tokyo, Prague, and Rio de Janeiro.

Act Four
The Apprehensive Fifties

THE HOT WAR of the nineteen-forties turned into the cold war of the nineteen-fifties. The race for military supremacy between the world's two great powers, and two opposing ideologies, brought fear and apprehension to the hearts of all. Government budgets zoomed as new and greater weapons had to be devised. Bomb-proof shelters were being built in American back yards, and cellars were being stocked with food and medicines in the event of a possible nuclear attack. Like an uncontrolled epidemic, brush-fire wars, guerrilla wars, undeclared wars, and wars disguised as police action erupted in different parts of the world at different times, all involving American resources and manpower. "Brinksmanship" became an ally of diplomacy as threats and counterthreats thundered from both the East and the West. Soon even outer space became an area for competition, as rockets and artificial satellites orbited the earth with equipment and men.

Anxiety, heightened tensions, the fear for tomorrow became the norm of life. There had to be escape from current realities and the ever-present dread of a future nuclear explosion if life was to be lived. Some of the books, movies, TV shows, stage productions, and songs of the nineteen-fifties met this need with flights into the nostalgic past or into fanciful dream worlds.

All of Cole Porter's musical comedies in the fifties provided such routes away from the grimness of an atomic age. This is probably why his songs were so good, and why they were so successful. For he always flourished creatively when he could write for escapist settings and plots.

Cole Porter's first musical comedy in the fifties tried to do for Greek legend what *Kiss Me, Kate* had done for Shakespeare. It was called *Out of This World*, was produced by Saint Subber and Lemuel Ayers on December 21, 1950, and had a cast headed by Charlotte Greenwood, who returned to the Broadway stage after almost a quarter-century absence. Once again, as in

Kiss Me, Kate, past and present were inextricably intertwined in the plot. The present was represented by an American couple come to Greece on a honeymoon; the past, by an adaptation of the old Amphitryon legend in which Jupiter tries to win away a young bride from her husband. And once again, as in *Kiss Me, Kate*, songs were beautifully integrated with story and characters. It was for the sake of integration that the best song Porter had created for his show had to be dropped from the production before it reached New York. "From This Moment On" was thrown out during out-of-town tryouts because it did not rise naturally from the situation in which it had been placed. It was published later as an independent number. The other songs, however, were inseparable from action and story. Some of them were "Use Your Imagination," "They Couldn't Compare to You" and "Where, Oh, Where."

To get into the Grecian spirit of *Out of This World*, Porter had gone to Athens in the late spring of 1950. He then traveled on a chartered yacht to the Aegean Sea among the Greek islands. This was his first trip abroad since his serious accident in 1937; and he was making it in spite of the fact that he was still victimized by its ravages, still suffered severe pain from time to time, still limped badly, still had to be helped in getting from one place to the next.

Just before that Grecian pilgrimage in search of local color and atmosphere, the Porters stopped off in Paris, their 1920 playground, to revive precious old memories.

Their one-time palatial home had long since been sold and was now a school. The Porters, therefore, took an apartment at the Ritz Hotel where for several weeks they held court. In between rounds of entertaining their friends, they made frequent excursions to old haunts—restaurants, bistros, night spots, cafés, art galleries.

It was a far different Paris now from the one they had known. In many ways the city was becoming more American than French. Paris now boasted cafeterias and luncheonettes to cater to the demands of those who were ready and willing to sidestep the traditional two-hour lunch. Now you could munch on frankfurter and roll if you wished, and drink Coca-Cola. You could have orange juice and ham and eggs for breakfast. You could listen to American hot jazz in smoke-filled cellars every night of the week or participate in the current American dances to the swing and sway of American bands.

The more Cole Porter saw how the face of Paris was changing, the more he was obsessed with nostalgia for the days gone by. And it was out of his own nostalgia that, back in America, he was able to create some of the most hauntingly Gallic, and some of the most distinctively Cole Porterian songs of his career—for two musical comedies with Parisian settings.

CAN-CAN WAS THE FIRST of Cole Porter's two Parisian musicals of the nineteen-fifties. It opened at the Shubert Theater on May 7, 1953, to enjoy the second longest run of any Cole Porter musical—892 performances. The "can-can" was, of course, the favorite nineteenth-century French dance in which a row of chorus girls delighted some (and shocked others) with their high kicks and provocative bodily contortions. Familiar since 1830, the can-can became the rage in Paris in the middle of the nineteenth century—especially after it had appeared in Offenbach's comic opera, *Orpheus in the Underworld*, where gods and goddesses of Mt. Olympus give it an abandoned performance. The can-can was subsequently denounced as immoral, and efforts were made to outlaw it. Indeed, toward the end of the nineteenth century, the dance had become legally tabu. Nevertheless, it was still being performed surreptitiously, mostly in out-of-the-way night spots in Montmartre—places that were intermittently raided by the police.

It was around one such effort to raid a Montmartre night spot that Abe Burrows, the librettist of *Can-Can*, spun a story line, placed in the year of 1893 in Montmartre. He created a text in which the colorful Paris of a bygone era came vividly to life: the Paris of Toulouse-Lautrec's paintings and posters; the Paris rhapsodized by Gustave Charpentier in his opera *Louise;* the Paris of the girlie-girlie shows at the Moulin Rouge.

The night spot providing the background for the action in *Can-Can* is one owned and operated by La Mome Pistache. A French judge, Aristide Forestier, is despatched to the place to investigate whether or not the illicit can-can is being performed there. Pistache works her charm on the judge until he falls completely in love not only with her but also with her night spot, and is ready and willing to close his eyes to any wrongdoings. In fact, Aristide is eager to use all his judicial influence and legal skill to clear the good name of the cabaret and its owner. And in the end, due to his efforts, the can-can is once again permitted to flourish in the open.

Lilo was imported from Paris to play the part of Pistache. Her engaging French accent (which reminded many in the audience of Irene Bordoni back in the days of *Paris*) and her spicy mannerisms and gestures contributed a good deal of Parisian sauce to the whole dish. But the performer who won the hearts of the audience completely—and who, by virtue of her electrifying dancing in this production, became a permanent star in the musical theater—was Gwen Verdon, also a newcomer to Broadway. Dances conceived by Michael Kidd were among the principal attractions of *Can-Can*, and most particularly a wild Apache dance, and a production number set in the Garden of Eden in which Gwen Verdon starred.

The piquant flavor of Paris were to be found in every facet of the production: in Jo Mielziner's wonderful sets, one of which, depicting the rooftops of Paris, inspired Porter's "I Love Paris"; the opening curtain on which was painted a design of the city with its crisscross of boulevards; the dances, especially the uninhibited can-can with which the musical comedy came to an exciting end.

No less Parisian were Porter's songs, not only "I Love Paris," but other numbers like "C'est magnifique," "Allez-vous en," "Montmart' " and "Can-Can"—each echoing and vibrating with Porter's own unforgettable memories of one-time Paris. Two other numbers, however, gave expression to Cole Porter's way of life and love whether in Paris or New York: "Live and Let Live" and "It's All Right with Me."

When, in 1964, *Show* magazine asked Richard Rodgers to single out one favorite among all of Cole Porter's songs his choice fell upon "It's All Right with Me." What impressed him most about the song was its altogether new approach to love by means of words and music. "Begin with the lyric. . . . These words present a basic reaction that all of us have experienced at one time or another—one of almost rueful pleasure. It's all simple and direct, but there's a fairly intellectual concept accompanying the emotion that makes for something refreshing and moving. To describe a tune in terms of its attractiveness is almost impossible, but this one with its crisscrossing of minor to major and the insistence of its rhythm makes it just about irresistible. With this song, Cole Porter never was better and there is no higher praise."

After its long successful run in the living theater, *Can-Can* came to the screen in 1960 in a big and magnificently produced star-studded show. Frank Sinatra, Shirley MacLaine, Maurice Chevalier, Louis Jourdan, and Juliet Prowse were in the cast. Even before the many delights of this film could burst from the Todd-A-O colored screen, *Can-Can* became news—front-page news— even international news. In 1959, Premier Khrushchev of the Soviet Union paid a visit to the United States. While in Hollywood, he was invited to the studios to watch a rehearsal of the can-can number. The dance routine shocked the Premier, who denounced it brusquely. His outraged criticism, of course, was publicized on the front pages of newspapers the world over and was responsible for piquing the interest of the movie-going public, not only in the dance but in the movie of which it was a segment.

THE COLE PORTER musical comedy following *Can-Can* was *Silk Stockings*, opening at the Imperial Theater on February 24, 1955 and staying there for a year and a half. Here, as in *Can-Can*, the setting is Paris, and the nostalgic flavor of the city as it once was is strong. This was a musical comedy derived by George S. Kaufman, Leueen McGrath, and Abe Burrows from *Ninotchka*, a nonmusical movie which had starred Greta Garbo in 1939 and was a satire on Soviet bureaucracy and officialdom. Ninotchka is a female Soviet agent of frozen emotions and disciplined political and social thinking. She is sent to Paris to retrieve a Soviet composer who had gone to the French capital to write the background music for a French screen adaptation of Tolstoy's *War and Peace*. In Paris, Ninotchka discovers her passionate espousal of the Soviet ideology and way of life wilting under the hot flame of French luxury, gaiety, and good living. At the same time her once-frozen emotions melt under the warmth of a romance with an American theatrical agent. Before long she becomes torn between her overwhelming desire to stay in Paris for good with the man she loves, and her duty to her country. Patriotism wins out. She returns to the Soviet Union. But her lover follows her there and finally persuades her to escape with him back to France.

The broad vein of satire that had previously been tapped in Cole Porter's musical comedy of the nineteen-thirties, *Leave It to Me*—where the subject matter was also of Soviet interest—once again yielded the rich blood of hilarious episodes and incidents. Ivanov, Brankov, and Bibinski—three blundering agents—come from Moscow to bring Ninotchka home, and provide a devastating caricature of Soviet officials. A bit of dialogue here, a passing remark there, are like incisive scalpels cutting deep into the flesh of Soviet life. One of the commissars asks for a copy of Who's Still Who—obviously the Soviet equivalent of Who's Who. When an American is told that the world-famous Soviet composer, Serge Prokofiev, is dead, he remarks in all innocence: "I didn't even know he had been arrested." Passing the buck of authority from a higher to a lower echelon becomes an accepted routine which all involved understand and submit to.

Cole Porter burlesqued Russian folk songs in "Too Bad" and "Siberia." He lampooned the movies in "Josephine" and "Stereophonic Sound." And he was at his best and most ingratiating whenever he spoke of Paris. Irony turned to gentle nostalgia, mockery to tenderness and romantic ardor, particularly in a song like "Paris Loves Lovers." There were also two fine love songs in the score, "Without You" and "All of You."

Brooks Atkinson placed *Silk Stockings* with the best of Cole Porter, and the best of Broadway. "It offers the wittiest dialogue of recent years, Cole Porter's best work and enormous gusto and skill in performance. . . . As in the most expert musical comedies, everything contributes to the vitality of everything else. The topic of Soviet dialectical earnestness has put Mr. Porter back in his best form. His music, with some clever burlesques of the Russian folk chorus, is bold, ironic and melodious with great variety in form. And his intricately worded lyrics rank with those earlier rhymes of his that have become part of the popular American culture. . . . But the best thing about it is the logic and wit with which the story weaves in and out of the spectacular and the smaller scenes, now and then exploding into the noisy revelry of ballets. . . . This [is a] humorously tempestuous show."

The other critics were also lavish with their praises. "*Silk Stockings*," wrote Robert Coleman in the *Daily Mirror*, "is a saucy, sexy, satiric saturnalia. . . . You'd better rush to the Imperial box-office right away if you want to relish it in the near future. For tickets to this wonderful laugh champ are going to be as hard to come by as ducats for the next World Series. Don't miss this delight. The town's newest musical magnet!"

Richard Watts, Jr., in the New York *Post*, found it to be a "vigorous, tuneful and often hilariously satirical show, which gives every sign of being a hit and . . . deserves to be."

Thirty-nine years—and twenty-four shows—after he had first hit Broadway, Cole Porter was still "the top."

DURING THE FIFTIES Cole Porter was represented on the screen by three musicals. One was the adaptation of *Silk Stockings*, in 1957, an M-G-M release starring Fred Astaire and Cyd Charisse in the role created for Broadway by Don Ameche and Hildegarde Neff. This was a lavish, bountiful, colorful production, made all the more delectable by several of Fred Astaire's inimitable dance creations, for which he had found a worthy partner in Cyd Charisse.

Two other screen musicals had original Cole Porter scores. In 1956, *High Society*, starred Bing Crosby, Grace Kelly, and Frank Sinatra in an M-G-M production. For Bing Crosby and Grace Kelly, Porter conceived a love ballad that became one of the year's great hits and which, from then on, was sometimes sung at American weddings together with the inevitable "Oh, Promise Me." The ballad was "True Love," and the Capitol recording by Crosby and Grace Kelly sold over a million disks.

In 1957, M-G-M released *Les Girls* with Gene Kelly and Mitzi Gaynor. Here we find one more of those Cole Porter songs which William K. Zinsser described in the New York *Herald Tribune* as a "moody, semi-Gallic ode to joy in gay Paree"; the song was called "Ça c'est l'amour."

Television was also enriched by Cole Porter's music—old songs as well as new. The old ones were heard in a ninety-minute production of the Ford Star Jubilee over the CBS network on October 6, 1956. A mighty procession of Cole Porter classics was sung and played to commemorate Porter's fortieth anniversary in show business.

New Cole Porter songs were heard in a television spectacle, *Aladdin*—a musical treatment of the famous tale from *The Arabian Nights*. This TV "special" was seen and heard on the Du Pont Show of the Month over CBS on February 21, 1958, with a cast headed by Anna Maria Alberghetti and Sal Mineo. Of the four songs Porter wrote for this lavish production the best was the love ballad shared by the stars and called "I Adore You."

In February of 1956, Porter chartered a yacht for a leisurely cruise from Lisbon to the Greek islands. He hoped that the Mediterranean sun and the beauty of the Greek islands in the Aegean would dispel the chill and gloom that had held him so long. Despite his successes in every area of the entertainment world; in spite of his wealth; in spite of his pride in his creative achievements; in spite of his lifelong capacity to enjoy so many things so zestfully—in spite of all this, Cole Porter's life in the nineteen-fifties was being darkened by ominous clouds portending a coming storm. His old injuries were again troubling him severely, but he had long since accustomed himself to live with pain. What afflicted him far more now was his terrible loneliness.

Linda Lee Porter had died in May, 1954. This was an irreplaceable loss, since through the years she had been not only his wife but also a beloved friend, an incomparable companion in good times, a comforting solace and support in difficult periods. He had never for a moment tried to envision what life would be for him without her ever-present grace, tenderness, stimulation, understanding, and admiration. He had long since come to accept these as part of his environment the way luxurious surroundings were. When he wrote "True Love" he touched on a new sensitive, genuine, and poignant strain both in words and music, such as he had never realized in his love ballads before this. In "True Love" he was speaking with simplicity, directness, and lack of affectation because the sentiment in that song came straight from his heart. This was surely the most deeply moving love song he had ever written; and it was moving because he wrote it soon after his wife's death, with the memory of the richness she had brought him fresh in his consciousness. He wrote in that song: "For you and I have a guardian angel on high, With nothing to do, But to give to you and to give to me, Love forever true." Surely in writing these lines he was thinking of the more than thirty years he had shared with Linda, now forever gone.

Whatever zest he still had for travel and sight-seeing, for exploring unfamiliar places or revisiting familiar ones, seemed to have died with her. He went from one locale to the next, with a weariness of spirit matched only by the fatigue of the flesh. He soon had to realize that for him there was no real escape from misery. And so he decided to go home to his empty apartment at the Waldorf-Astoria. And there he sank more deeply than ever into melancholia, and suffered increasing torment from the stabbing pains in his right leg.

He was taken back to the hospital in 1958 for further tests and possibly for more surgery. His physicians finally reached a grim diagnosis. Porter's chronic *osteomyelitis*—a bone tumor—demanded the amputation of the leg if his life was to be spared.

They saved his life when they removed that leg at the Harkness Pavilion of the Columbia Presbyterian Medical Center in New York on April 3, 1958. But they could not save his spirit, his will to work, and his will to live.

Epilogue
The Tragic Sixties

NEAR-TRAGIC AND tragic events were calculated to try man's soul in the first half of the sixties: the Cuban crisis that carried the world to the edge of a nuclear holocaust; the Berlin wall; the assassination of President Kennedy; the sweep of communism across southeast Asia; the eruption of racial tensions in America into outright violence; the sharp rise throughout the country in juvenile delinquency and crime.

But there was also a good deal happening in the early nineteen-sixties to inspire hope: the expanding rift between Moscow and Peking which shattered the unity of the Communist world; the passage in America of the strongest Civil Rights bill since Reconstruction; the completion of a nuclear-test ban, the first sign of a possible thaw in the cold war; manned orbital space flights promising eventual landings on the moon; the momentous reign of Pope John XXIII and the convening of the Twenty-first Ecumenical Council seeking ways and means of achieving Christian unity and world peace. . . .

For Cole Porter, however, those years brought no alterations of light and shade, only the darkness of hopeless despair. After his leg had been amputated, he sank ever deeper into desolation. This man who had once loved life so passionately, and had lived it with such intensity, was now rejecting it. He had built around himself a wall through which neither friends, nor admirers, nor social pleasures could penetrate. Isolation and seclusion became his way of life. After attending one party at the home of a close friend, where he overheard somebody whisper, "Poor, poor Cole," as he was being carried in, he refused ever again to attend parties, or to visit his friends, or to go to first nights in the theater. No longer did his apartment hum with the bright voices of the many who had enjoyed spending an evening with him.

Worst of all, he had no further appetite for writing

songs or working on shows. *Silk Stockings* in 1955 had been his last Broadway show; *Les Girls*, in 1957, his last original score for the movies; *Aladdin*, for TV, in 1958, his last assignment in any medium. After *Aladdin* his creative life came to a sharp halt in the same way as his social life had done.

He still clung to one or two old habits. June 11 remained the day on which he left for his California home; and on weekends he still visited his place in Williamstown, Massachusetts. But if this was meant to be an escape, it proved an escape only from one setting to another. The loneliness, the abject misery followed Porter wherever he went.

Attended by his faithful secretary, Madeline P. Smith, and two valets who served him around the clock, Porter's life after 1958 was reduced to bare essentials—to no more than the mere motions of survival. He dozed until about noon. After being dressed, he partook of a sparing lunch in his secretary's room, tasting this or that, but eating very little. He then was carried to his car for a short drive in the city for about half an hour.

For a while he faithfully attended a rehabilitation hospital in an effort to learn how to use an artificial limb, aided by two canes. But by 1963 he gave up all hope of ever learning to walk again, surrendered to defeat, and henceforth depended for his transportation on his valets, who carried him.

Late-afternoon naps were followed by a drink. Porter then dressed for dinner (his wardrobe still meticulously correct, the carnation still in the lapel). One of Porter's friends, or a couple, might be invited for dinner—but no more than that. These visitors came with the hope of trying to lift him from his despondency, but to no avail. Despite their presence, he spoke little if at all. His chin was sunk into his neck, his eyes were half closed. He hardly ever touched the succulent dishes placed before him. When the guest or guests departed—and usually they went early—Cole Porter was left with his bitterness and his memories until he was carried to bed.

Though a recluse, Porter was not forgotten by the grateful world outside which stood ever ready to hail him for the unique place he had won for himself both in American popular music and in the American musical theater. On May 15, 1960, there took place at the Metropolian Opera House in New York a "Salute to Cole Porter." A "glittering array of stars" was heard in songs that made Porter's legend in his own lifetime. The evening began with William Gaxton's rendition of "You're the Top" and "You Do Something to Me." It ended with twelve of America's most celebrated popular composers at twelve pianos, directed by Richard Rodgers, in a presentation of "Begin the Beguine." In between, Beatrice Lillie sang "Love for Sale"; Celeste Holm, "True Love"; Lilo, "I Love Paris"; Lisa Kirk, "Always True to You in My Fashion." Harold Lang, a group headed by Bambi Linn, and a glee club all joined forces for "Night and Day." Several outstanding stage personalities including Arlene Francis, Faye Emerson, Howard Lindsay, and Bella Spewack served as "emcees." "The Porter music shone through with an unusual glow," reported *Variety*. All Broadway, all Tin Pan Alley seemed to be in attendance. There was one glaring omission—Cole Porter had refused to come. All the proceeds from this evening—about $65,000—went to charity, to the Children's Asthma Research Institute and Hospital.

Less than a month after that, Porter received an honorary doctorate of Humane Letters from Yale University. Since he refused to attend Commencement ceremonies where this degree was to be conferred, a delegation from Yale visited him on June 9, 1960, at his apartment. This was the first time that Yale ever conferred an honorary degree *in absentia*. There Provost Norman S. Buck hung a velvet hood on him. "As an undergraduate," said the Provost in a brief ceremony, "you first won acclaim for writing the words and music of two of Yale's annual football songs. Since then you have achieved a reputation as a towering figure in the American musical theater."

Nor did his friends and associates forget to celebrate his seventieth birthday on June 9, 1962. They all gathered on the stage of the Orpheum Theater at St. Marks and Second avenues in downtown, New York (where *Anything Goes* was then being successfully revived). There a giant midnight birthday party took place, even though the composer was not present. Elsa Maxwell was the mistress of ceremonies. Champagne flowed. Cole Porter numbers were sung. As a band struck up other tunes, some people started doing the

Twist in the aisles. Then the hundreds upon hundreds of performers, composers, lyricists, producers and other friends and colleagues who knew and loved Porter joined their voices in chanting "Happy Birthday" as a seven-tiered birthday cake was being cut. It was the kind of party Cole Porter would once have delighted in. That night he was home—alone.

He remained completely withdrawn after that—withdrawn from his work, from the theater, from his friends, from pleasures once enjoyed. He could taste the full bitterness of lines he had once written for a song for *Kiss Me, Kate*: "Where is the fun I used to find? Where is it gone? Gone with the wind!"

If, on June 11, 1964, he made the trip with his entourage from New York to his home in California, it was only because he was far too weary of spirit to break a long-standing habit. In the past he had gone to California with anticipation and exhilaration; there were *so* many good friends there whose company he enjoyed. This time he went weighed down by despair—and crushed by inner fears that seemed to hint darkly that he was making this trip for the last time and that he would never again come back to New York.

He never did come back. Suffering severe pain, this time from a kidney stone, he had to be operated upon at the Santa Monica Hospital, on October 13, 1964. It was not a difficult operation, or a serious one, and it went well. Nevertheless it marked the end for Cole Porter—because he had no further wish to live. When

Cole Porter died in that hospital on October 15, 1964, at 11:05 P.M., his physicians reported that he had "simply stopped breathing." His body had finally surrendered, just as his spirit had done earlier.

He died as he had been living for the past few years —alone. His only surviving relatives (two cousins) were miles away. No friend was present. His chauffeur and valet were outside the hospital room. The only one near him when he breathed his last was a comparative stranger, his nurse.

In his song, "Blow, Gabriel, Blow," Cole Porter had written: "I've gone through brimstone and I've been through fire." It was true—he *had* gone through fire and brimstone, but death had finally released him from his suffering.

Appendixes

1916

See America First. Book by T. Lawrason Riggs. Starring Clifton Webb. Maxine Elliott Theatre, March 28, 1916. 15 performances. SONGS: Buy Her a Box at the Opera; Ever and Ever Yours; I've a Shooting Box in Scotland; The Language of Flowers; Lima.

1919

Hitchy-Koo of 1919. Book by George V. Hobart. Starring Raymond Hitchcock, Lillian Kemble Cooper, Florence O'Denishawn, and Joe Cook. Liberty Theatre, October 6, 1919. 56 performances. SONGS: I Introduced; Hitchy's Garden of Roses; When I Had a Uniform On; Peter Piper; My Cozy Little Corner in the Ritz; Old-Fashioned Garden; That Black and White Baby of Mine; Another Sentimental Song; I've Got Somebody Waiting.

1924

Greenwich Village Follies. Additional lyrics by Irving Caesar and John Murray Anderson. Starring the Dolly Sisters, Vincent Lopez and his orchestra, and Moran and Mack. Shubert Theatre, September 16, 1924. 127 performances. SONGS: I'm in Love Again; Britanny; My Long-Ago Girl; Make Ev'ry Day a Holiday; Wait for the Moon.

1928

Paris. Book by Martin Brown. Starring Irene Bordoni. Music Box Theatre, October 8, 1928. 195 performances. SONGS: Don't Look at Me That Way; Two Little Babes in the Woods; Vivienne; Let's Do It; Heaven Hop; Let's Misbehave; Quelque Chose; Which.

1929

Fifty Million Frenchmen. Book by Herbert Fields. Starring William Gaxton and Genevieve Tobin. Lyric Theatre, November 27, 1929. 254 performances. SONGS: You Do Something to Me; You've Got That Thing; Find Me a Primitive Man; The Happy Heaven of Harlem; You Don't Know Paree; I'm in Love; I'm Unlucky at Gambling; Paree, What Did You Do to Me?; Let's Step Out; I Worship You; Please Don't Make Me Be Good; The Queen of Terre Haute.

Wake Up and Dream. Book by J. H. Turner. Starring Jack Buchanan and Jessie Matthews. Selwyn Theatre, December 30, 1929. 136 performances. SONGS: Wake Up and Dream; I Loved Him, but He Didn't Love Me; The Banjo That Man Joe Plays; What is This Thing Called Love?; Looking at You; I'm a Gigolo; Agua Sincopada, Tango; I Want to be Raided by You; I Dream of a Girl in a Shawl.

1930

The New Yorkers. Book by Herbert Fields based on a story by Peter Arno and E. Ray Goetz. Starring Hope Williams, Charles King, and Clayton, Jackson and Durante. Broadway Theatre, December 8, 1930. 168 performances. SONGS: Where Have You Been?; I'm Getting Myself Ready for You; Love for Sale; The Great Indoors; Take Me Back to Manhattan; Let's Fly Away; I Happen to Like New York; Just One of Those Things (*not* the famous one).

1932

Gay Divorce. Book by Dwight Taylor. Starring Fred Astaire and Claire Luce. Ethel Barrymore Theatre, November 29, 1932. 248 performances. SONGS: After You;

Night and Day; How's Your Romance?; I've Got You on My Mind; Mister and Missus Fitch; You're in Love.

1934

Anything Goes. Book by Guy Bolton, P. G. Wodehouse, Howard Lindsay, and Russel Crouse. Starring William Gaxton, Ethel Merman, and Victor Moore. Alvin Theatre, November 21, 1934. 420 performances. SONGS: I Get a Kick Out of You; All Through the Night; You're the Top; Anything Goes; Blow, Gabriel, Blow; Buddie, Beware; Waltz Down the Aisle; The Gypsy in Me; There'll Always Be a Lady Fair.

1935

Jubilee. Book by Moss Hart. Starring Mary Boland and Melville Cooper. Imperial Theatre, October 12, 1935. 169 performances. SONGS: Why Shouldn't I?; The Kling-Kling Bird on the Divi-Divi Tree; When Love Comes Your Way; Begin the Beguine; A Picture of Me Without You; Me and Marie; Just One of Those Things (the famous one).

1936

Red, Hot and Blue. Book by Howard Lindsay and Russel Crouse. Starring Ethel Merman, Jimmy Durante, and Bob Hope. Alvin Theatre, October 29, 1936. 183 performances. SONGS: Ours; Down in the Depths; You've Got Something; It's De-Lovely; A Little Skipper from Heaven Above; Ridin' High; The Ozarks Are Calling Me Home; Red, Hot and Blue; Goodbye, Little Dream, Goodbye; You're a Bad Influence.

1938

You Never Know. Book by Rowland Leigh adapted from Siegfried Geyer's play *Candle Light.* Starring Clifton

Webb and Libby Holman. Winter Garden, September 21, 1938. 78 performances. SONGS: Maria; You Never Know; What Is That Tune?; For No Rhyme or Reason; From Alpha to Omega; What Shall I Do?; At Long Last Love.

Leave It to Me. Book by Bella and Samuel Spewack based on their play *Clear All Wires.* Starring William Gaxton, Victor Moore, and Sophie Tucker. Imperial Theatre, November 9, 1938. 307 performances. SONGS: I'm Taking the Steps to Russia; Get Out of Town; Most Gentlemen Don't Like Love; From Now On; I Want to Go Home; My Heart Belongs to Daddy; Tomorrow; Far, Far Away.

1939

Du Barry Was a Lady. Book by Bud De Sylva and Herbert Fields. Starring Bert Lahr and Ethel Merman. 46th Street Theatre, December 6, 1939. 408 performances. SONGS: Ev'ry Day a Holiday; When Love Beckoned in Fifty-Second Street; Come on In; But in the Morning, No!; Do I Love You?; Give Him the Oo-La-La; Well, Did You Evah!; It Was Written in the Stars; Katie Went to Haiti; Friendship.

1940

Panama Hattie. Book by Bud De Sylva and Herbert Fields. Starring Ethel Merman and James Dunn. 46th Street Theatre, October 30, 1940. 501 performances. SONGS: Visit Panama; My Mother Would Love You; I've Still Got My Health; Fresh as a Daisy; Who Would Have Dreamed?; Let's Be Buddies; Make It Another Old-Fashioned, Please; All I've Got to Get Now Is My Man.

1941

Let's Face It. Book by Herbert and Dorothy Fields adapted from *Cradle Snatchers,* a play by Russell Medcraft and

Norma Mitchell. Starring Danny Kaye and Eve Arden. Imperial Theatre, October 29, 1941. 547 performances. SONGS: Jerry, My Soldier Boy; Farming; Ev'rything I Love; Ace in the Hole; You Irritate Me So; Rub Your Lamp; Let's Not Talk About Love; A Little Rumba Numba; I Hate You, Darling.

1943

Something for the Boys. Book by Herbert and Dorothy Fields. Starring Ethel Merman and Bill Johnson. Alvin Theatre, January 7, 1943. 422 performances. SONGS: See That You're Born in Texas; When My Baby Goes to Town; Something for the Boys; Could It Be You?; Hey, Good-Lookin'; He's a Right Guy; The Leader of a Big-Time Band; I'm in Love with a Soldier Boy; By the Mississinewah.

1944

Mexican Hayride. Book by Herbert and Dorothy Fields. Starring Bobby Clark and June Havoc. Winter Garden, January 28, 1944. 481 performances. SONGS: Sing to Me, Guitar; The Good Will Movement; I Love You; There Must Be Someone for Me; Carlotta; Girls; Abracadabra; Count Your Blessings; It Must Be Fun to Be You.

Seven Lively Arts. Book by Moss Hart, George S. Kaufman, Ben Hecht and others. Starring Beatrice Lillie and Bert Lahr. Ziegfeld Theatre, December 7, 1944. 183 performances. SONGS: Is It the Girl?; Ev'ry Time We Say Goodbye; Only Another Boy and Girl; Wow-Ooh-Wolf; When I Was a Little Cuckoo; Frahngee-Pahnee; Hence, It Doesn't Make Sense; The Band Started Swinging a Song.

1946

Around the World. Book by Orson Welles adapted from

the novel of Jules Verne. Starring Arthur Margetson and Julie Warren. Adelphi Theatre, May 31, 1946. 74 performances. SONGS: Look What I Found; There He Goes, Phileas Fogg; Should I Tell You I Love You?; Pipe Dreaming; If You Smile at Me; Wherever They Fly the Flag of Old England.

1948

Kiss Me, Kate. Book by Bella and Samuel Spewack based on Shakespeare's *The Taming of the Shrew.* Starring Alfred Drake, Patricia Morison, Lisa Kirk, and Harold Lang. Century Theatre, December 30, 1948. 1,077 performances. SONGS: Another Op'nin', Another Show; Why Can't You Behave?; Wunderbar; So in Love; We Open in Venice; Tom, Dick or Harry; I've Come to Wive It Wealthily in Padua; I Hate Men; Were Thine That Special Face; I Sing of Love; Too Darn Hot; Where is the Life that Late I Led?; Always True to You in My Fashion; Bianca; I Am Ashamed that Women Are So Simple; Brush Up Your Shakespeare.

1950

Out of This World. Book by Dwight Taylor and Reginald Lawrence based on the Amphitryon legend. Starring Charlotte Greenwood. Century Theatre, December 21, 1950. 157 performances. SONGS: Use Your Imagination; Where, Oh Where?; I Am Loved; Climb Up the Mountain; No Lover; Cherry Pies Ought to Be You; Hark to the Song of the Night; Nobody's Chasing Me; From This Moment On; You Don't Remind Me.

1953

Can-Can. Book by Abe Burrows. Starring Lilo and Peter Cookson. Shubert Theatre, May 7, 1953. 892 performances. SONGS: Never Give Anything Away; C'est Magnifique; Come Along With Me; Live and Let Live; I Am in Love; If You Loved Me Truly; Montmart'; Allez-vous En; It's All Right with Me; I Love Paris; Can-Can.

1955

Silk Stockings. Book by George S. Kaufman, Leueen MacGrath, and Abe Burrows. Starring Don Ameche and Hildegarde Neff. Imperial Theatre, February 24, 1955. 477 performances. SONGS: Paris Loves Lovers; Stereophonic Sound; It's a Chemical Reaction; All of You; Satin and Silk; Without Love; As on Through the Seasons We Sail; Josephine; Siberia; Silk Stockings.

II. MOTION-PICTURE PRODUCTIONS

1929

Battle for Paris (Paramount). Starring Gertrude Lawrence. SONGS: They All Fall in Love; Here Comes the Band Wagon.

1931

Fifty Million Frenchmen. (Warner). A screen adaptation of the musical comedy. Starring William Gaxton and Helen Broderick. The basic stage score was used.

1934

Wake Up and Dream (Universal). A screen adaptation of the musical comedy. Starring Russ Columbo, June Knight, and Roger Pryor. SONG: What Is This Thing Called Love?

The Gay Divorcee (RKO). A screen adaptation of the

musical comedy, *The Gay Divorce*. Starring Fred Astaire and Ginger Rogers. SONG: Night and Day.

1936

Born to Dance (M-G-M). An original screen score. Starring Eleanor Powell and James Stewart. SONGS: Love Me, Love My Pekinese; Easy to Love; Hey, Babe, Hey!; Rap Tap on Wood; I've Got You Under My Skin; Rolling Home; Swingin' the Jinx Away.

Anything Goes (Paramount). A screen adaptation of the musical comedy. Starring Bing Crosby and Ethel Merman. SONGS: Anything Goes; All Through the Night; You're the Top; Blow, Gabriel, Blow; There'll Always Be a Lady Fair; I Get a Kick Out of You.

1937

Rosalie (M-G-M). An original screen score. Starring Nelson Eddy and Eleanor Powell. SONGS: In the Still of the Night; I've Got a Strange New Rhythm in My Heart; Close; Who Knows; Rosalie; Why Should I Care?

1940

Broadway Melody of 1940 (M-G-M). An original screen score. Starring Fred Astaire and Eleanor Powell. SONGS: Between You and Me; Please Don't Monkey with Broadway; I Concentrate on You; I've Got My Eyes on You; I Happen to Be in Love.

1941

You'll Never Get Rich (Columbia). An original screen score. Starring Fred Astaire and Rita Hayworth. SONGS: Boogie Barcarolle; Shootin' the Works; Since I Kissed My Baby Goodbye; So Near and Yet So Far; The Wedding Cakewalk; Dream Dancing.

1942

Something to Shout About (Columbia). An original screen score. Starring Don Ameche and Janet Blair. SONGS: I Always Knew; Something to Shout About; You'd Be So Nice to Come Home To; Hasta Luego; It Might Have Been; Lotus Bloom.

Panama Hattie (M-G-M). A screen adaptation of the musical comedy. Starring Ann Sheridan and Red Skelton. SONG: Fresh as a Daisy.

1943

I Dood It (M-G-M). Starring Red Skelton and Eleanor Powell. SONG: Swinging the Jinx Away.

Du Barry Was a Lady (M-G-M). A screen adaptation of the musical comedy. Starring Red Skelton, Gene Kelly and Lucille Ball. SONGS: Do I Love You?; Katie Went to Haiti; Friendship.

Let's Face It (Paramount). A screen adaptation of the musical comedy. Starring Bob Hope and Betty Hutton. SONG: Let's Not Talk About Love.

1944

Hollywood Canteen (Warner). An all-star cast including Jack Benny, Eddie Cantor, Bette Davis, and others. SONG: Don't Fence Me In.

1946

Night and Day (Warner). A screen biography of Cole Porter starring Cary Grant as the composer. The score was made up entirely of Cole Porter standards. SONGS: In the Still of the Night; Old-Fashioned Garden; Let's Do It; You Do Something to Me; Miss Otis Regrets; What Is

This Thing Called Love?; I've Got You Under My Skin; Just One of Those Things; You're the Top; I Get a Kick Out of You; Easy to Love; My Heart Belongs to Daddy; Begin the Beguine; Night and Day.

1948

The Pirate (M-G-M). An original screen score. Starring Judy Garland and Gene Kelly. SONGS: Nina; Mack the Black; You Can Do No Wrong; Love of My Life; Be a Clown.

1949

Adam's Rib (M-G-M). Starring Katherine Hepburn. SONG: Farewell, Amanda.

1950

Stage Fright (Warner). Starring Marlene Dietrich. SONG: The Laziest Gal in Town (written in 1927).

1952

Kiss Me, Kate (M-G-M). A screen adaptation of the musical play. Starring Kathryn Grayson and Howard Keel. The basic stage score was used.

1956

High Society (M-G-M). An original screen score. Starring Bing Crosby, Grace Kelly, and Frank Sinatra. SONGS: Little One; Who Wants to Be a Millionaire?; True Love; You're Sensational; I Love You, Samantha; Now You Have Jazz; Mind If I Make Love to You?

Anything Goes (Paramount). A screen remake of the musical comedy. Starring Bing Crosby, Donald O'Connor and Mitzi Gaynor. The basic stage score was used.

1957

Les Girls (M-G-M). An original screen score. Starring Gene Kelly, Kay Kendall, and Mitzi Gaynor. SONGS: Les Girls; Ça, c'est amour; Why Am I So Gone About That Gal?; You're Just Too, Too!

Silk Stockings (M-G-M). A screen adaptation of the musical comedy. Starring Fred Astaire and Cyd Charisse. The basic stage score was used.

III. TELEVISION PRODUCTION

1958

Aladdin. Book by S. J. Perelman based on a tale from *A Thousand and One Nights.* Starring Anna Maria Alberghetti and Sal Mineo. Du Pont Show of the Month (CBS). SONGS: Trust Your Destiny to a Star; Opportunity Knocks But Once; Aladdin; I Adore You.

IV. COLE PORTER'S GREATEST SONGS

Ace in the Hole. Introduced by Mary Jane Walsh, Sunny O'Dea, and Nanette Fabray in *Let's Face It.*

Allez-vous En. Introduced by Lilo in *Can-Can.*

All of You. Introduced by Don Ameche in *Silk Stockings.*

All Through the Night. Introduced by Bettina Hall and William Gaxton in *Anything Goes.*

Always True to You in My Fashion. Introduced by Lisa Kirk in *Kiss Me, Kate.*

Anything Goes. Introduced by Ethel Merman in *Anything Goes.*

Begin the Beguine. Introduced by June Knight in *Jubilee.*

Blow, Gabriel, Blow. Introduced by Ethel Merman in *Anything Goes.*

By the Mississinewah. Introduced by Ethel Merman and Paula Laurence in *Something for the Boys.*

C'est Magnifique. Introduced by Lilo and Peter Cookson in *Can-Can.*

Come Along With Me. Introduced by Erik Rhodes and Hans Conried in *Can-Can.*

Don't Fence Me In. Introduced by Roy Rogers in *Hollywood Canteen.*

Easy to Love. Introduced by Frances Langford in *Born to Dance.*

Find Me a Primitive Man. Introduced by Evelyn Hoey in *Fifty Million Frenchmen.*

Friendship. Introduced by Ethel Merman and Bert Lahr in *Du Barry Was a Lady.*

From This Moment On. Introduced by Priscilla Gillette and William Eythe in *Out of This World.*

Get Out of Town. Introduced by Tamara in *Leave It to Me.*

I Concentrate on You. Introduced by Douglas MacPhail in *Broadway Melody of 1940.*

I Get a Kick Out of You. Introduced by Ethel Merman and William Gaxton in *Anything Goes.*

I Hate Men. Introduced by Patricia Morison in *Kiss Me, Kate.*

I Love Paris. Introduced by Lilo in *Can-Can.*

I Love You. Introduced by Wilbur Evans in *Mexican Hayride.*

In the Still of the Night. Introduced by Nelson Eddy in *Rosalie.*

It's All Right with Me. Introduced by Peter Cookson in *Can-Can.*

It's De-Lovely. Introduced by Ethel Merman and Bob Hope in *Red, Hot and Blue.*

I've Got You on My Mind. Introduced by Fred Astaire and Claire Luce in *Gay Divorce.*

I've Got You Under My Skin. Introduced by Virginia Bruce in *Born to Dance.*

Just One of Those Things. Introduced by June Knight and Charles Walters in *Jubilee.*

Katie Went to Haiti. Introduced by Ethel Merman in *Du Barry Was a Lady.*

Let's Be Buddies. Introduced by Ethel Merman and Joan Carroll in *Panama Hattie.*

Let's Do It. Introduced by Irene Bordoni and Arthur Margetson in *Paris.*

Let's Misbehave. Introduced by Irene Bordoni in *Paris.*

Live and Let Live. Introduced by Lilo in *Can-Can.*

Love for Sale. Introduced by Kathryn Crawford in *The New Yorkers.*

Old-Fashioned Garden. Introduced by Lillian Kemble Cooper in *Hitchy-Koo of 1919.*

Mister and Missus Fitch. Introduced by Luella Gear in *Gay Divorce.*

My Heart Belongs to Daddy. Introduced by Mary Martin in *Leave It to Me.*

Night and Day. Introduced by Fred Astaire and Claire Luce in *Gay Divorce.*

Paris Loves Lovers. Introduced by Don Ameche and Hildegarde Neff in *Silk Stockings.*

Rosalie. Introduced by Nelson Eddy in *Rosalie.*

So in Love. Introduced by Patricia Morison in *Kiss Me, Kate.*

True Love. Introduced by Bing Crosby and Grace Kelly in *High Society.*

Two Little Babes in the Wood. Introduced by Irene Bordoni in *Paris.*

Were Thine That Special Face. Introduced by Alfred Drake in *Kiss Me, Kate.*

What Is This Thing Called Love?. Introduced by Frances Shelley in *Wake Up and Dream.*

Wunderbar. Introduced by Alfred Drake and Patricia Morison in *Kiss Me, Kate.*

You'd Be So Nice to Come Home To. Introduced by Janet Blair and Don Ameche in *Something to Shout About.*

You Do Something to Me. Introduced by William Gaxton and Genevieve Tobin in *Fifty Million Frenchmen.*

You Irritate Me So. Introduced by Nanette Fabray and Jack Williams in *Let's Face It.*

You're the Top. Introduced by Ethel Merman and William Gaxton in *Anything Goes.*

You've Got Something. Introduced by Jack Thompson and Betty Compton in *Fifty Million Frenchmen.*

You've Got That Thing. Introduced by Jack Thompson and Betty Compton in *Fifty Million Frenchmen.*

V. SELECTED RECORDINGS

Stage, Screen, and TV Productions

Aladdin. Original cast: Columbia CL-1117.

Anything Goes. Soundtrack: Decca 8318; also Mary Martin, chorus and orchestra: Columbia ML-4751.

Broadway Melody of 1940. Soundtrack. M-G-M E-3590.

Can-Can. Original cast: Capitol W-452; Soundtrack: Capitol W-1301.

High Society. Soundtrack: Capitol W-750.

Kiss Me, Kate. Original cast: Columbia OL-4140; Soundtrack: M-G-M, 3077.

Panama Hattie. Ethel Merman and orchestra: Decca A-203.

Les Girls. Soundtrack: M-G-M 3590.

Mexican Hayride. Members of original New York production: Decca DL-5232.

Out of This World. Original cast: Columbia ML-4390.

The Pirate. Soundtrack: M-G-M E-21.

Silk Stockings. Original cast: Victor LOC-1016; Soundtrack: MGM-3542.

Miscellaneous Song Collections

Harry Arnold. The Music of Cole Porter: Riverside 7536.

Ben Bagley. Cole Porter Revisited. Fourteen "rediscovered" songs assembled by Ben Bagley: RIC-3002.

Frank Chacksfield. The Best of Cole Porter: Richmond 20066.

Buddy Cole. Buddy Cole Plays Cole Porter: Warner 1226.

Ella Fitzgerald. The Porter Song Book: Verve 4001-2; Ella Fitzgerald Sings Cole Porter: Verve 4049; Ella Fitzgerald Sings More Cole Porter: Verve 4050.

Morton Gould. Kern and Porter: Victor LM-2559.

Allan Jones: Night and Day Album: Victor M-1033.

André Kostelanetz. Music of Cole Porter: Columbia CL-729.

Mary Martin. Cole Porter Songs: Decca A-123.

Heinz Neubrand. Porter and Kern: Amadeo 9081.

Cyril Ornandel. The Musical World of Porter: M-G-M 4843.

Raoul Poliakin. The Music of Gershwin and Porter: Everest 5051.

David Rose. Cole Porter Revue: Victor P-158.

Risë Stevens. Songs of Cole Porter: Columbia MM-630.

Individual Songs

Ace in the Hole. Hildegarde: Decca 23242.

Allez-vous En. Kay Starr: Capitol EAP 1-482.

Begin the Beguine. Artie Shaw Orchestra: Victor 20-1752;

also Frank Sinatra: Columbia 37064; also Bing Crosby: Decca 23972.

By the Mississinewah. Paula Laurence and Betty Garrett: Decca 23363.

C'est Magnifique. Gordon MacRae: Capitol EAP 1-482.

Come Along With Me. Sarah Vaughan: Mercury 70331.

Don't Fence Me In. Bing Crosby and the Andrews Sisters: Decca DX-151.

Easy to Love. Johnny Mathis: Columbia CL-887; also Dinah Shore: Victor LPM-1154.

Friendship. Judy Garland and Johnny Mercer: Decca 3165.

Get Out of Town. Artie Shaw and orchestra: M-G-M X-1043.

I Concentrate On You. Dinah Shore: Victor LPM-1154.

I Love Paris. Bing Crosby: Decca DL-5520; also Tony Martin: Victor 47-5535.

In the Still of the Night. Risë Stevens: Columbia 7549-M.

It's All Right with me. Lena Horne: Victor 47-6175; also Sammy Davis, Jr.: Decca DL-8710.

It's De-Lovely. Ethel Merman: Decca A-681.

I've Got You Under My Skin. Frank Sinatra: Capitol W-653.

Just One of Those Things. Les Brown Orchestra: Columbia 50045.

Katie Went to Haiti. Mary Martin: Decca 23150.

Let's Do It. Noel Coward: Columbia ML-5063.

Love for Sale. Tommy Dorsey Orchestra: Victor LPM-22.

My Heart Belongs to Daddy. Mary Martin: Decca 11041; also Peggy Lee: Decca DL-5482.

Night and Day. Fred Astaire: Label X-LUA-1001; also Benny Goodman Orchestra: Columbia CL-524.

Rosalie. Artie Shaw Orchestra: Victor LPT-28.

What Is This Thing Called Love? Percy Faith Orchestra: Columbia CL-6203.

You'd Be So Nice to Come Home To. Frank Sinatra: Capitol W-803.

You Do Something to Me. Perry Como: Victor LPM-1085; also Frank Sinatra: Columbia CL-6143.

VI. A SELECT BIBLIOGRAPHY

"Cole Porter, The Professional Amateur." *Time*, January 31, 1949.

"Cole Porter, From Venice to Can-Can in Thirty Years." *Newsweek*, May 18, 1953.

The Cole Porter Song Book. New York: Simon and Schuster, 1959.

Ewen, David, *Panorama of American Popular Music*. New York: Prentice-Hall, 1957.

Ewen, David, *Popular American Composers*. New York: H. W. Wilson Co., 1962.

Green, Stanley, *The World of Musical Comedy*. New York: Ziff-Davis, 1960.

Harriman, Margaret Case, "Cole Porter: A Profile." *New Yorker*, November 23, 1940.

Hart, Moss, "Cole Porter." *Harper's*, September 1959.

Kreuger, Miles, "From Fame to Fortune." *The American Record Guide*, May, 1959.

Lounsberry, Fred (editor), *103 Lyrics of Cole Porter*. New York: Random House, 1954.

Maxwell, Elsa. *R.S.V.P.: Elsa Maxwell's Own Story*. Boston: Little Brown, 1954.

Merman, Ethel, *Who Could Ask For Anything More?* New York: Doubleday, 1955.

Millstein, Gilbert, "Words And Music by Cole Porter." *New York Times Magazine*, February 20, 1955.

Rudel, Julius, "And Nobody Missed the Waltz." *Theatre Arts*, June 1956.

Smith, Cecil, *Musical Comedy in America.* New York: Theatre Arts, 1950.

Spaeth, Sigmund, *A History of Popular Music in America.* New York: Random House, 1948.

"Words and Music by the Top." *New York Times Magazine*, June 9, 1963.

INDEX